Successor journal to *Theatre Quarterly* (1971–1981)
VOLUME XVI   PART 2   (NTQ 62)

MAY 2000

Editors
CLIVE BARKER
SIMON TRUSSLER

Advisory Editors: Arthur Ballet, Eugenio Barba, Susan Bassnett, Tracy Davis, Martin Esslin, Maggie Gale (*Book Reviews Editor*), Lizbeth Goodman, Peter Hepple, Ian Herbert, Jan Kott, Brian Murphy, Maria Shevtsova, Sarah Stanton, Juliusz Tyszka, Ian Watson

Contents

New Theatre Quarterly is published in February, May, August, and November by Cambridge University Press, The Edinburgh Building, Shaftesbury Road, Cambridge CB2 2RU, England   ISBN 0 521 78902 8   ISSN 0266 – 464X

Editorial Enquiries

Oldstairs, Kingsdown, Deal, Kent CT14 8ES, England (e-mail: simon@country-setting.co.uk)

Unsolicited manuscripts are considered for publication in *New Theatre Quarterly*. They should be sent to Simon Trussler at the above address, but unless accompanied by a stamped addressed envelope (UK stamp or international reply coupons) return cannot be guaranteed. Contributors should follow the journal's house style as closely as possible. A style sheet is available on request.

Subscriptions

New Theatre Quarterly (ISSN: 0266-464X) is published quarterly by Cambridge University Press, The Edinburgh Building, Shaftesbury Road, Cambridge CB2 2RU, UK, and The Journals Department, 40 West 20th Street, New York, NY 10011-4211, USA.

Four parts form a volume. The subscription price, which includes postage (excluding VAT), of Volume XVI, 2000, is £55.00 (US$90.00 in the USA, Canada and Mexico) for institutions, £32.00 (US$50.00) for individuals ordering direct from the publishers and certifying that the Journal is for their personal use. Single parts cost £15.00 (US$25.00 in the USA, Canada and Mexico) plus postage. EU subscribers (outside the UK) who are not registered for VAT should add VAT at their country's rate. VAT registered subscribers should provide their VAT registration number. Prices include delivery by air. Japanese prices for institutions are available from Kinokuniya Company Ltd., P.O. Box 55, Chitose, Tokyo 156, Japan.

Orders, which must be accompanied by payment, may be sent to a bookseller or to the publishers (in the USA, Canada and Mexico to the North American Branch). Periodicals postage paid at New York, NY, and at additional mailing offices. POSTMASTER: send address changes in the USA, Canada and Mexico to *New Theatre Quarterly*, Cambridge University Press, The Journals Department, 110 Midland Avenue, Port Chester, NY 10573-4930, USA.

Claims for missing issues will only be considered if made immediately on receipt of the following issue.

Information on *New Theatre Quarterly* and all other Cambridge journals can be accessed via http://www.cup.cam.ac.uk/ and in North America via http://www.cup.org/.

The Edinburgh Building, Cambridge CB2 2RU, United Kingdom
40 West 20th Street, New York, NY 10011-4211, USA
10 Stamford Road, Oakleigh, Melbourne 3166, Australia

Typeset by Country Setting, Kingsdown, Deal, Kent CT14 8ES
Printed and bound in the United Kingdom at the University Press, Cambridge

Russell Jackson

Staging and Storytelling, Theatre and Film: 'Richard III' at Stratford, 1910

The film of F. R. Benson's company in scenes from *Richard III*, released in 1911 and now available on the BFI's *Silent Shakespeare* video, was shot on stage in Stratford-upon-Avon, using stock scenery from the Memorial Theatre. Because of this, it is a unique document of Shakespearean production in the period, exemplifying the uneasy relationship between stage and film. The settings can be documented from a number of other sources: the original designs; a photograph of the stage set with the medieval street which appears in two episodes; and a series of postcards – the latter apparently 'production stills' of the film. *Macbeth*, *The Taming of the Shrew*, and *Julius Caesar* were also filmed, but have not survived, though the Stratford archives contain some photographic evidence of them. Russell Jackson is Deputy Director of the Shakespeare Institute, the University of Birmingham's graduate school of Shakespeare studies in Stratford-upon-Avon. Recently he has published a translation of a work by Theodor Fontane, *Shakespeare in the London Theatre, 1855–58* (Society for Theatre Research, 1999), and he is editor of the forthcoming *Cambridge Companion to Shakespeare on Film*.

THE ORIGINAL Shakespeare Memorial Theatre in Stratford-upon-Avon, predecessor of the Royal Shakespeare Theatre, opened in 1879 and was destroyed by a fire in 1926. The film of F. R. Benson's company in *Richard III*, released in 1911, was shot on its stage and using the theatre's stock scenery.[1] Although it has been dismissed as 'stage film at its worst',[2] and can hardly be claimed as a contribution to the advancement of the cinema, this *Richard III* is none the less a valuable theatrical document. It offers a unique view of an Edwardian theatre company at work in a theatre, with the scenery used for regular performances there; but the nature of its relationship to the theatre calls for further examination.

With three other films of the same troupe on the same stage (*Julius Caesar*, *The Taming of the Shrew*, and *Macbeth*), *Richard III* was issued in 1911 by the Co-operative Cinematograph Company.[3] In a studio, lighting conditions could usually be controlled by combining available sunlight with powerful arc lamps, and during the years leading up to the First World War more and more studios were filming exclusively with artificial light.[4] The Memorial Theatre, with its compact stage, offered conditions not dissimilar to those of contemporary studios. During the first decades of cinema it was not unusual for film companies to transport the sets and properties of a theatre production to their studios, or to reproduce the sets with appropriate adjustments (as in the 1913 *Hamlet*, with Forbes-Robertson.) But filming a production on the stage of a theatre appears to have been unusual.

The Scenery of the Film

The stage settings used in *Richard III* can be summarized as follows:

1. *Battle of Tewkesbury*. Backcloth of distant landscape, framed (on cloth) by trees to the viewer's left and right.

2. *Murder of Henry VI*. Patterned backing (stone walls, with tapestry), with practicable door set close against it at an angle on right.

3. *Richard sets the King against Clarence*. Backdrop of street scene. Practicable steps and rostrum (leading off) placed upstage extreme right, apparently close to cloth. Market cross with square 'stone' base upstage left.

4. *Funeral procession and wooing*. As 3.

5. *Murder of Clarence.* Stone wall flats at rear, with open archway at centre, backed with a curtain. Immediately in front of arch, centre-stage and set parallel to the backdrop, is a bed on a rostrum with steps, which are covered with a plain stage-cloth.

6a. *King Edward is told of Clarence's death: he himself dies.* Centre arch as in 5, but with backing (cloth or flat?) of stone arches in perspective instead of curtain. Flat with 'stone' arch angled against it on left. Throne on low rostrum with tapestry backing set at an angle on right.

6b. *Princes arrive.* As 6a.

6c. *Hastings sent to execution.* As 6a but with council table on right of screen.

7. *Lord Mayor offers the crown.* As 6c.

8. *Richard, now king, discards Buckingham, and orders death of princes.* As 6a/b.

9. *Murder of Princes.* As 5, but with bed upstage left of centre: oblong trap open immediately behind it, for murderer to descend.

10. *Richmond in England.* Woodland backcloth, with 'cottage' wing set close against it on extreme right (onstage edge only is visible).

11. *Richard on his way to meet Richmond.* Street scene as 3, but without rostrum and steps on right. Cross now set upstage right.

12. *Dream.* Landscape backcloth (river in distance) with tent opening set against it, upstage left. The ghosts appear on a rostrum in front of the tent, and Richard's bed and table are set upstage across centre.

13. *Bosworth.* Forest backcloth, with matching cut cloth about two feet immediately in front of it. A forest wing is set about four feet in front of this on the left-hand side. (No wing is visible on the right.)

These settings employ items identifiable in an album of watercolour designs for the theatre's stock of scenery.[5] From plans of the building, newspaper reports, and the few extant photographs of Stratford stage settings *in situ*, it is possible to form some impression of the way this stage scenery was adapted for filming. Additional evidence is provided by four murky snapshots taken by the theatre's librarian, W. Salt Brassington, which show what has been assumed to be a rehearsal for *Julius Caesar, c.* 1909.[6]

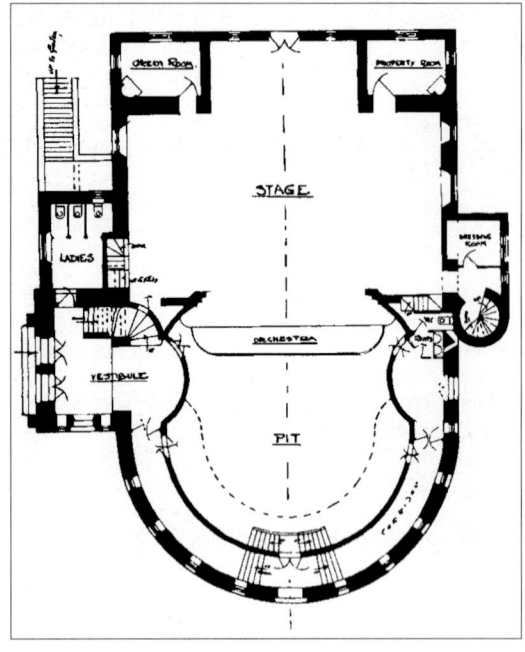

Staging for the Camera

The stage of the Memorial Theatre, which opened in 1879, was notoriously small (see plan above). The partial circle of its auditorium (now occupied by that of the Swan Theatre) faced a conventional proscenium arch stage, with a shallow forestage and an orchestra pit. A contemporary report, amounting to a press release from the theatre's governors, suggests the pride with which its appointments were regarded. The stage was provided 'with all the latest appliances and improvements, and [would] be found to meet the requirements of any piece however elaborate in its scenic effects' (*Stratford-upon-Avon Herald*, 17 January 1879).

The proscenium was 26 ft wide and 27 ft 6 ins high. The stage area was reported to be 46 ft deep from the footlights to the back: evidently this was the measurement along the centre line to the rear wall of the stage dock. The plan shows areas on either side of the 'stage dock' designated 'Property or star dressing room' (opposite prompt side) and 'Green room etc' (prompt side) and projecting some 10 ft forward from the back wall. These narrowed the scene dock's width to about 24 ft. From the resulting 36 ft of depth, a few feet must be subtracted to allow

Top: view of the auditorium and stage of the Shakespeare Memorial Theatre, showing the 'Street Scene' set in position, *c.* 1910. Bottom: the death of King Edward, with a 'crafty-looking Richard feeling his pulse', in one of the postcards of the Benson Company's *Richard III*. (Photos by courtesy of Shakespeare Centre Library.)

for crossing behind the scenes. Effectively, much less than 30 ft of stage depth would normally have been available.

Comparison of the plan with the photograph indicates that the forestage was about 5 ft deep from proscenium arch to orchestra pit, but that at least half of this was taken up by the footlights and the protective wires in front of them. This further reduced the usable area upstage of the proscenium arch to little more than 25 ft deep. According to the newspaper announcement, the stage was to be 53 ft wide. This measurement is of the architectural space, from one wall to the other: the practicable acting area, allowing for the wings, would have been about 20 ft wide.

Given these approximate measurements, and making further allowance for sightlines (even assuming that many spectators would have only a partial view of the stage picture), little of the stage's depth was in fact available for significant action. It would have been unwise to transact any important business of the play outside a triangular space with its base at the curtain line and its apex 12 ft or so upstage on the centre line.

The photograph of the stage with the street scene, reproduced on the previous page, gives a clear sense of the restrictions. The top of the back cloth is in shadow in the photograph of the fully set stage, but it appears that some 15 ft of its height would have been visible from the stalls. (In the film and the postcards, actors standing on the stage floor against the backcloth reach the top of the ground-floor level of the painted houses on the left-hand street corner, suggesting a maximum of 6 ft above stage level for this point on the cloth.)

In the 1909 photographs of *Julius Caesar*, the shot taken from the front (opposite, top) shows the speaker's rostrum and the back cloth of the forum scene as respectively no more than 12 and 15 feet upstage of the proscenium line. This estimate seems to be confirmed by a pencil note in a Benson Company promptbook for this play, which indicates 'bottom of pulpit [immediately upstage of the bier] 11 feet from Act Drop.'[7] The second photograph (opposite, bottom), is looking across the stage into the wings from a position under the proscenium arch, and shows the front of a 'tent' exterior positioned about as far back.

The *Herald* report on the stage appointments indicated that there would be 'five wing entrances' on either side. Counting entrances back from the proscenium, this would require four scenic wings on each side. This suggests that the photograph of the street scene shows the stage set to its fullest depth. On the audience's left (i.e., opposite prompt) side four wings are set: alternating houses and shrubbery (possibly the onstage edge of 'woodland' wings), with the house wings downstage.

The front 'house' wing is set close to the furled tableau curtain immediately behind the proscenium arch, and the rearmost wing (woodland) is very close to the backcloth. On the boarded stage the outlines of five traps are visible, with an oblong 'grave' trap centre stage, between the lines of the first and second wings. The newspaper report mentions four 'star' traps, one 'great grave trap', one 'Corsican slider', and three 'bridge cuts', and announces that 'The whole of the stage is being constructed so as to open whenever [*sic*: wherever?] necessary, with slides to take off running underneath the wing sides.'

In other words, each section of floor could be pulled off in two segments, dividing at the centre so that the halves could slide under the floor on either side of the stage. No borders are visible above the stage (perhaps because the photograph was taken from the first circle level, prompt side) but what appears to be the lower edge of the act drop shows behind the tableau curtains, and casts a shadow onto the back of the scene. The 1879 newspaper report stated that the act drop would be on a roller, and the curtain would 'rise and form drapery at the top of the proscenium'.

Adapting Stage for Film

For all its limitations, the stage of the Memorial Theatre was in fact not dissimilar in its effective acting area from those commonly available in film studios – where, according to one contemporary account, 'the scene itself occupie[d] but a small space, generally about 12 or 16 feet in width', with the camera 'brought within a few feet of the picture, in order that the actors [might] be photographed as large as possible'.[8]

'Murky snapshots' by W. Salt Brassington, apparently showing rehearsals for *Julius Caesar*. Top: the forum scene, showing the speaker's rostrum. Bottom: the 'tent' exterior, at far left of the photograph. (By courtesy of the Record Office, Shakespeare Birthplace Trust.)

If we turn to the film's settings, we can form some impression of the way the stage and its resources have been adapted. In one episode of the film (Scene 10: Richmond in England), wings are placed upstage, very close to the back cloth. In these open-air scenes the acting area in front of the camera is probably somewhat shallower than it would normally have been for performances on the full stage of the theatre.

In the final scene, however, the back cloth, cut cloth, and wing seem to be set further apart. This may be because, unlike the flats forming wall segments, the cloths had to be hung in available flying positions. In the more confined interiors (Scenes 2, 5, and 9) the stone arch and flats (and the practicable door in Scene 2) are set close together, forming a trapezoid acting area with the longest side closest to the camera.

For the murder of the princes, an episode not included in stage performances, use is made of the rectangular 'grave' trap. The bed is placed between it and the camera and the flats are set some 18 inches behind the trap's upstage edge, which seems to have been no more than 6 feet behind the curtain line. However, the precise arrangement of the flats in these scenes may reflect film rather than stage practice. Intending 'photo-play' writers were advised that the cinema image removed two imaginary walls where the stage took away only one, and that 'action must be concentrated between two walls of a room set at right angles'.[9]

We can surmise, then, that the filming required some compression of the stage space for outdoor scenes, and the adoption of customary theatre staging for the interiors, both 'Palace' and 'Tower', perhaps with some adjustment of the flats representing walls. At its deepest, the stage space used for the film seems to be formed by bringing the back of the scene forward, down to the line of the third, 'house' wing from the front in the street-scene photograph. In scenes where a stage cloth is used, its front edge is visible in the foreground, and marks the forward boundary of the action. In the photograph of the street scene, we can see approximately 4 to 6 feet of the left-hand side of the backcloth (up to the doorway of the corner house) that is not shown in Scenes 3 and 11 of the film.

The Theatre's Scenic Stock

Like the theatre's stage, the scenery in question may have been on a small scale, but like the other appointments of the Memorial (comprising theatre, gallery, and library) it was the best that money, aided by generosity, could obtain. In a review of *The Merry Wives of Windsor* on 29 April 1887, the *Stratford-upon-Avon Herald* noted that 'The Memorial Theatre is obtaining quite a reputation for pretty scenery.' The street cloth itself received admiring notices when it was first seen, in the 1886 *Richard III* performances. The correspondents of both the *Evesham Journal* (24 April) and the *Stratford-upon-Avon Herald* (30 March) praised its subtlety of colour and the *trompe-l'oeil* modelling, the former declaring: 'A better canvas I have not seen in any provincial town.' The *Herald* noted the skill with which 'a cross placed at the entrance to the street greatly enhances its effect' – presumably the movable (and slightly wobbly) market cross, seen in the film.

Comparison of the watercolour design in the Royal Shakespeare Company's archive (opposite) with the photograph of the set on stage (page 109, top) shows that the backcloth was executed more or less faithfully. The stone cross on the right was omitted and the arrangement of windows and gables on the same side was altered slightly, together with the window pattern of the house as glimpsed on the extreme left (only just 'on' in the stage photograph). The angle and perspective of the design seem to have been adhered to, with more or less the same area of painted street surface between the buildings and the stage floor.

Some of the scenes in the album are referred to in the minute book of the theatre's governing body, although as it happens none of those in the film are mentioned. At their meeting on 13 December 1878 the governors of the Memorial Theatre commissioned a drop-scene from William Beverley, who asked for £50, half his usual fee.[10]

Watercolour design by John O'Connor for stock English street scene (Shakespeare Centre).

The following January, in preparation for the opening season, they accepted an estimate from Mr. F. Lloyds, an eminent scenic artist, for settings appropriate to the two plays to be presented, *Much Ado About Nothing* and *Hamlet*. The minutes of the meeting of 31 January 1879 show that the artist was to receive £250 and the carpenters £150, the whole to be paid in weekly instalments. The scenery was to be delivered by 3 April.

In 1880 more scenery was commissioned, to accommodate three new revivals (*The Merchant of Venice*, *The Lady of Lyons*, and *The School for Scandal*). The chairman announced that 'the extra Scenery . . . could be done by Mr. [John] O'Connor and Mr. Lloyds at an estimate of about £250' (23 March 1880). In 1889 O'Connor is referred to again, as having 'kindly undertaken the direction of the scenery' for a performance of the *First Part of Henry VI* – the programme for which credits

O'Connor with designing the scenery, and L. W. Hall with painting it, although Henry Irving is thanked for his kindly loan of 'the Abbey scene'.

A few other items in the theatre's scenic stock – notably the 'Saxon' stone walls and archway – can be further documented from photographs, but none are as informative as the image of the street scene. Photographs of the set stage from the period of the old theatre (1879–1926) are rare in the archive, and most publicity shots (often in postcard format) are portraits of performers in costume, taken against the ivy by the theatre's entrance door. In the case of *Richard III*, however, some scenes are illustrated by four postcards which correspond closely to the staging adopted for the film, if not exactly to its action.

For example, in the film we do not see Richard with a prince on either side of him, or his 'beheading' gesture as he consigns

113

Buckingham to execution (both reproduced above), while the page in the background of the latter scene is further to the right of the film camera. But the postcards do seem unusually close to the film in other respects. All the scenes correspond to episodes in the film. Unlike most stage photographs of the period, these are 'action' shots, and do not seem to have been posed specially for a still camera.

In the scene of Hastings being consigned to execution (opposite page, top), a file of soldiers in the background is shown just after they have made a right turn in order to march off, and some of the court ladies in the scene with Richard and the princes are caught glancing towards the camera. The even lighting, with its careful avoidance of shadows, may reflect that set up for the film,

in which powerful 'purple' lights (described to J. C. Trewin forty years later by one of the actors) were set up, presumably augmenting the theatre's electric stage lighting.[11] On film – and in the street scene photograph – the edges of the scenery and stage cloths and the lines of the boards are mercilessly exposed. Facial expressions and costume are sharper in the cards than in the film, and the still camera seems to have been closer to the actors.

The archive's four postcards of *Richard III* are labelled on the original with a roman numeral in the bottom right-hand corner: the highest number is 'XIII', which suggests they are survivors from a larger set. If they are indeed related to the film, it is possible that the surviving items from two other sets of postcards of the same kind represent the staging of the lost films of other plays. Two postcards of *Macbeth* (one of which is reproduced below) show scenic elements that appear in the film and in the photographs of *Richard III* – the 'Saxon' arches and stone walls that in accord with nineteenth-century

theatrical custom would have served for *Hamlet*, *Lear*, and *Macbeth* and other plays with a medieval setting.

Two postcards of *The Taming of the Shrew*, apparently numbered 5 and 6 of a set, show 'Italianate' scenery (architectural elements, landscape background, as in the one reproduced opposite, top), resembling designs in the album. Other features suggest that these represent 'stills' of scenes from lost films: the action is confined to the same stage area as appears in both the film and the postcards of *Richard III*, and the lighting, and depth and sharpness of focus, also correspond. Another card for *The Taming of the Shrew* (opposite, bottom) shows the final scene, with a formal comic line-up of couples across the front; but the crowd in the background does not seem to have been posed carefully and specifically for a still shot.

The Play's Action on Stage

Since 1886 F. R. Benson and his company had been the mainstay of the Stratford spring and summer festival seasons, lending the Memorial Theatre a sense of participation in national theatrical life, and a distinctive role. It thus avoided the fate that had threatened it in the years immediately following its opening – of becoming no more than a site for occasional theatrical acts of homage on Shakespeare's birthday, and a receiving house for miscellaneous provincial tours (not by any means a number one venue) for the rest of the year.

The Benson Company's work and its participation in the life of Stratford-upon-Avon have been well documented, and Frank Benson's influence as a trainer of actors and a vigorous and idealistic exponent of popular Shakespeare are widely acknowledged. At the same time, it has to be admitted that the production values of his company were often poor, and that even for the 1900s his notions of Shakespearean performance were old-fashioned. This was actor-managerial theatre, offering a recognizably 'traditional' style of production. The film reflects this, as well as illustrating such commonplace practices of the time as the playing of children

and young men by women *en travestie* (the princes, and the page who accompanies Richard in Scene 11) and the introduction of picturesque details of local colour (the dancing children in Scene 3.)

Historians have decried the film as hopelessly theatrical – in Rachel Low's words, 'a simple photographic record' of episodes in a theatrical performance – but it is clear that the action of the play has been rethought to make it intelligible in cinematic terms. Some episodes have been contrived specifically for the film: Richard is seen poisoning King Edward's mind against Clarence (with the help of a cowled monk); the crown is on stage in two scenes (Scenes 6c, 7) to make Richard's ambition clear, and in another (6b) so that he can prevent the crowning of the Prince of Wales; King Edward obligingly dies on stage (the postcard on page 109 shows a crafty-looking Richard feeling his pulse); and the murder of the princes is shown.

Not all these pantomime episodes would be intelligible without a knowledge of at least the main events, and some (poisoning King Edward's mind) are still pretty obscure. But we should remember that the film's original exhibitors could expect audiences to possess a fair degree of at least anecdotal acquaintance with the story, and perhaps some experience of it in the theatre. Popular paintings (such as Millais' *The Princes in the Tower*, 1878) and illustrations of the play itself had reinforced this.[12]

The 'Henry VI' Interpolations

In one respect, the film's compressed narrative reflects a more controversial theatrical tradition: the inclusion of scenes from plays in the *Henry VI* sequence. The use of such material appears to have been initiated by Colley Cibber's adaptation of 1700, and the custom of opening *Richard III* with expository scenes, culminating in the murder of Henry VI, continued after other features of Cibber's text had been discarded.[13] By 1910, the date of the film's production, the Benson company had performed *Richard III* at Stratford – usually for no more than one performance – in the annual summer festivals of

Two postcards from *The Taming of the Shrew* set. Top: the road to Petruchio's house, against an Italianate land-scape. Bottom: the final tableau, an 'unposed' crowd suggesting a still from the film. (Shakespeare Centre Library.)

1886, 1887, 1894, 1897, 1899, 1901, 1906, 1908, and 1910; and from the programmes and reviews one can gather something of the nature of the text used.

Benson appears to have included the death of King Henry in seven out of these nine seasons. In 1886 the programme for the performance announces the play as being performed 'from Shakespeare's text' and King Henry does not appear in the cast list. This seems also to have been the case in 1887, but in 1894, although the programme makes no mention of the character, Benson gave playgoers a surprise. The reviewer in the *Leamington Spa Courier* (28 April 1894) was taken aback:

The opening scene . . . caused no little amazement, especially among those provided with copies of the work, for it was a scene taken, for some reason or other, from the middle of *Henry VI*, and introduced as a kind of melo-dramatic poem [sic: 'proem'?] to *Richard III*. This was certainly a rather curious liberty to take with Shakespeare's text in his own temple.

The reporter, clearly unsure of himself in the text of the *Henry VI* plays, notes that 'to make matters worse' the scene was given with such realism that the audience's reaction 'became little short of absolute repulsion before the curtain rolled down'. Gordon Crosse, a diligent and perceptive diarist of Shakespearean performances between 1890 and 1953, had seen Benson's company in the play at the New Theatre, Oxford, in 1893, but made no mention of the murder scene. In 1901 he saw the play again at Stratford, with the scene introduced, and noted that

we discover Henry in the Tower and he delivers the 'shepherd' speech, which is transposed from II.5 of 3 Hen VI, and loses much of its point by the transposition. Then the murder scene is played.

He observed wryly that 'Mr. Benson seems to think that by omitting Margaret altogether . . . he compensates for the introduction of her husband', and while praising Mr. Herbert's playing of the king for 'skill and pathos', he felt that he was 'too vigorous at the last'.[14]

In 1897 Henry had appeared again in Stratford, played by 'Mr. Edwards', an actor not otherwise listed in the season's programmes (perhaps a disguised doubling). In 1899 he was played by Mr. O. Tidman, who also appeared as Nym in *Merry Wives* and the First Murderer in *Macbeth*. Neither performance of the scene seems to have occasioned any comment in the papers. In 1906, when the sequence (or 'cycle') of history plays included the Second Part of *Henry VI* but neither of the other two, it seems that the murder scene was included again in *Richard III*. The *Stratford-upon-Avon Herald* commented that 'the end of Henry VI is painful, and Mr. Benson (as Richard) spares us no horror in his power' (11 May 1906).

In 1908, in a performance that included the guest star Genevieve Ward as Margaret, Henry was killed again, this time in the person of Stanley Howlett (although the list of scenes, probably erroneously, omits the 'prison in the Tower' required) and in 1909, when Guy B. Rathbone played the part, the programme informed audiences that 'Act 1 is preceded by a scene from *Henry VI, Part 3*'.

Reviews of these performances rarely make any mention of the scenery and stage appointments, beyond observing that they were adequate and appropriate. But a rare glimpse of the colourful costuming is given by the *Stratford-upon-Avon Herald's* observation on 28 April 1911 that Benson 'formed an impressive figure as seated on the throne, sumptuously arrayed in purple robes' – a useful reminder that spectacle would have been brightened even on this modest stage by the accurate and vividly coloured heraldry on which actor-managers of the time (including the relatively impecunious Benson) prided themselves. The *Standard* (29 April 1901) noted that 'the scenes laid in Richmond's tent were taken in a wood near Bosworth', and in 1894 the Leamington Spa *Courier* mentions the ghosts appearing to Richard *outside* his tent, as they do in the film.

It is clear from the lists of the acts and scenes and their locations included in some (but not all) of the theatre programmes that the play began either in a room (or prison) in the Tower, or in a street, depending on which version was given. At no time did the play begin with the battle scene shown in the film. No promptbook survives for the Stratford performances of *3 Henry VI* when all three parts were played in the 1906 season, and consequently there is no evidence of how the Battle of Tewkesbury had been staged by Benson, or whether then (as in the film) a real horse had been brought on stage! (If it was, the reviewers did not mention it.)

Benson's 'Points'

Unless there was some unusual contingency (such as Genevieve Ward's participation) the hard-worked local journalists did not take much notice of the familiar *Richard III*, beyond mentioning the relative effectiveness of the cast, but there was always a note of admiration for Benson's vigour and for the ever-popular sword-fight at the end. Benson was also praised for the 'realism' of his portrayal, which was even (as we have seen) considered excessive by some tender-nerved critics. Viewers of the film a century later may like to compare their reactions to Benson with those of the *Stratford-upon-Avon Herald* on 21 April 1899:

He brought out with rare skill the various phases of the character – his harsh, cruel disposition, the crafty cunning of his nature, his devilish humour, his religious hypocrisy. And though these were so clearly shown as to be unpleasant to contemplate in their extreme naturalness, they compelled the admiration of the house for the art which enabled the actor to so ably delineate them.

They may, however, find they have more in common with Crosse, whose 1901 diary entry notes that the performance does not show the company to much advantage, this being such a one-actor piece, and that Richard is in any case 'a part in which Mr. Benson's mannerisms run riot'. These were manifested in 'extreme loudness of voice and accompanying grimaces'.

He is by no means to be blamed for not following Sir H. Irving's comic intellectual Richard [*which Crosse had seen and admired in 1897*], but that is at least interesting, and Mr. Benson fails to supply the deficiency with anything really good. The ruling note of his performance is to be sharp and forcible. . . . His grim callous humour is not misplaced, e.g. when he wipes his sword on the murdered Henry's coat [*in the opening scene*], and then introduces one of his feats of strength by lugging the body out by the heels over his shoulder.[15]

One of Benson's most remarkable 'points' in the film is the playing of the wooing scene with Lady Anne, whom he appears to charm with looks and passes of his hand. Crosse thought this 'mesmerizing business' – later repeated with Elizabeth – 'overdone'.[16]

The eye-witness accounts of the filming quoted by J.C. Trewin describe the somewhat frantic compression of the scenes. The actors hurried from cue to cue under glaring lights with the 'producer' shouting instructions at them, in a manner quite different from their usual performance or rehearsal practice, but in fact (though neither informant mentions this) the rule in film-making at the time. The circumstances, and Benson's lack of experience before the camera, help to explain how little of the 'realism' of Benson's performance is still discernible.[17] At times, the gestures and facial expressions seem to be appropriate to the pace of the original (as in the wooing scene and in particular the 'mesmerism' moments) and a telling piece of business has been preserved in what must have been its original tempo.

One would like to know whether all of the stage business was regularly seen in the theatre: Richard's return to the council table to take a strawberry (it seems) after condemning Hastings; his scattering money for street children in the first street scene; or the wounded solider who drags himself upstage during the concluding combat to grasp a flag so that he can wave it behind the triumphant Richmond – none of these is mentioned by the observant Crosse. On the other hand there is no sign in the film (perhaps because of the compression of the action) of the 'mesmerizing' of Elizabeth as well as Anne, or of another startling innovation mentioned by Crosse: Richard's off-handedly killing a sleeping sentinel outside his tent after the dream sequence.

Crosse does however record two details seen in the film. One is Richard's continuing to fight Richmond with his left arm after the right was wounded. The other is Benson's variation of one traditional 'point', to which Crosse's notes on the 1893 Oxford performance add a detail necessarily absent on silent film: after the scene with the citizens Richard 'flung away his prayer book with one hand and his beads with another [as in the film], uttering an exultant cry of "King".'[18]

'Richard III' and the Status of the Cinema

Quite apart from its cinematic significance, the film of *Richard III* is a document of the stage business and the performance style of Benson and his company around 1910, and of the stage sets of the Shakespeare Memorial Theatre, although both action and stage space have been compressed. The production also exemplifies the lowly standing of film in its time. First, no mention was made of it or of the other films in the local newspapers, in the minutes of the theatre's governors, or in their published annual reports. This was a non-event as far as Stratford-upon-Avon was concerned.

Secondly, I have not been able to find records of any kind of payment for the films in the theatre's documents or in the Benson Company accounts for 1910–1911 (now in the Shakespeare Centre Library). The projected four-week festival was cut short after the performance of *The Merchant of Venice* on 6 May 1910 by the death of King Edward.

Manvell was told that filming of one play had been done in the mornings of a whole week when the company was performing at night, which seems to rule out the otherwise reasonable suggestion that Benson was allowed to make the films in the theatre that year as a way of making up the lost income. Perhaps it was simply assumed by the governors or their chairman that any profit from so inconsiderable an enterprise could be allowed to go to the actor and his company as a matter of course? It seems that, in that age of relative cinematic innocence, no kudos or profit was thought likely to accrue to the theatre itself. It is hard to imagine any arts organization or theatre company taking such a view nine decades later.

Around this *Richard III* clusters intriguing photographic evidence – what of the process of its making can be deduced from the film itself; the photograph of the street scene on stage (and the original scene designs); the postcards of *Richard III* and the other plays; and the *Julius Caesar* snapshots. I have suggested that the postcards may represent 'stills' from two of the missing films. The *Julius Caesar* photographs may be even more significant, although the conjecture here is less confident. [19]

The three rows of lights strung across the front of the stage seem unusually powerful and numerous for a rehearsal, and are positioned, like most film lighting of the time, to cast a very strong light from the front. The number of men in street clothes among the costumed actors seems considerable – more than would be customary at a rehearsal? William Salt Brassington, F.S.A. (1858–1939), the librarian at the Memorial Theatre, was otherwise liberal in the use of his portable camera and systematic in keeping the results: he seems not to have photographed any other scenes in the theatre he was attached to.[20] Was this a special occasion both for the theatre and for him? No film camera is visible in any of the pictures, but the forum scene photograph shows lines (tapes?) converging somewhere below the photographer's position. Are these marks to indicate the limits of the on-stage action, and are these perhaps photographs of the *making* of the lost film of *Julius Caesar*?

Notes and References

I am grateful for the enthusiasm and support of the archival and photographic staff of the Shakespeare Centre Library and the Records Office of the Shakespeare Birthplace Trust, and for suggestions by colleagues and students at the Shakespeare Institute, particularly Mary Allen, Lauren Bergquist, and John Jowett. All illustrations in this article are reproduced by kind permission of the Shakespeare Birthplace Trust.

1. The BFI's video *Silent Shakespeare* (BFI VO46) was issued in Spring 1999. *Richard III* was originally released in 1911, and appears to have been made in 1910, although the evidence for this is not conclusive. The notes accompanying the video, by Luke McKernan, give 1911 as the film's date and the video transfer is headed – probably wrongly – with the theatre's 1911 cast list, which is also included in *Walking Shadows* (see below). On the film itself, see Kenneth S. Rothwell and Annabelle Henkin Melzer, *Shakespeare on Screen: an International Filmography and Videography* (London, 1990), p. 237–8 (No. 498); Luke McKernan and Olwen Terriss, *Walking Shadows: Shakespeare in the National Film and Television Archive* (London, 1994), p. 136; Robert Hamilton Ball, *Shakespeare on Silent Film: a Strange Eventful History* (London, 1968), p. 84–8, 322–33; Rachel Low, *The History of the British Film, 1906-1914* (London, 1949). On the Shakespeare Memorial Theatre: Marian J. Pringle, *The Theatres of Stratford-upon-Avon, 1875-1992: an Architectural History* ('Stratford-upon-Avon Papers', No. 5, Stratford-upon-Avon, 1994); Sally Beauman, *The*

Royal Shakespeare Company: a History of Ten Decades (Oxford, 1982); J. C. Trewin, *Benson and the Bensonians* (London, 1960).

2. Ball, *Shakespeare on Silent Film*, p. 83. Like other commentators, Ball draws attention to the film's technical limitations: it consists largely of 'incomprehensible illustrations of subjects described by titles, of unrecognizable people doing unintelligible things'.

3. Low has no precise date for the release of *Richard III*, but indicates release dates for *Julius Caesar* (25 March 1911), *Macbeth* (9 April), and *The Taming of the Shrew* (22 April). The BFI copy of *Richard III* is 1,324 ft long: Low lists it as 'two reels', and gives lengths of 1,120 ft and 1,360 ft for the *Shrew* and *Macbeth* respectively, but no figure for *Julius Caesar* (*The History of the British Film. 1906-1914*, Appendix).

4. On filming techniques and conditions *c.* 1910–14 and the use of scenery from stage productions of plays, see Rachel Low, *The History of the British Film, 1906-1914* (London, 1949) and *1914-1918* (London, 1950.) As Low observes, the fixed camera and one-shot-per-scene composition of this film are primitive, even for 1910.

5. Album of scene designs, Shakespeare Centre Library, Stratford-upon-Avon. Some designs have been removed for display, and a stock list corresponding to the album's contents appears to have been lost. It nevertheless constitutes an impressive and unusual record of the stock scenes needed in the period for the production of the standard repertoire (Shakespeare, 'old English comedy', and the odd Victorian play). John O'Connor (who died in 1888, aged 58) was at one time 'stock scene-painter under [J. B.] Buckstone at the Haymarket' in the mid-1860s, and was the uncle of the scenic artist Joseph Harker, who refers to him in his *Studio and Stage* (London, 1924). See Richard Southern, 'Scenery at the Book League', *Theatre Notebook*, V (1950–51), p. 35–8.

6. Other photographs of stage settings in the old theatre include the scenes from *Richard II* and *As You Like It* reproduced by Beauman (both plays) and Trewin (*Richard II*). Few of the portrait photographs show stage scenery, although Trewin reproduces (opposite page 128) an image of Benson as King Lear in front of one of the stock stone wall flats. The four snapshots taken by the theatre's librarian, W. Salt Brassington, showing what has been assumed – quite reasonably – to be a rehearsal for *Julius Caesar*, *c.* 1909, are in the collection of his papers in the Record Office of the Shakespeare Birthplace Trust, files DR860/176–9. Gordon Crosse's *Shakespearean Playgoing, 1890–1952* (London, 1953) includes one of the *Richard III* postcards (Richard and the princes).

7. Benson Company *Julius Caesar* promptbook, Shakespeare Centre Library, 72.915. John Ripley, in '*Julius Caesar' on Stage in England and America, 1599–1973* (Cambridge, 1980), reproduces (p. 187) another photograph of the company, clearly rehearsing the forum scene – but not, it seems, at Stratford.

8. Frederick A. Talbot, *Moving Pictures: How They are Made and Worked*, 'Conquests of Science' series (London, 1912), p. 114.

9. Low, *The History of the British Film, 1914–1918*, p. 225.

10. Shakespeare Memorial Theatre, Governors' Minutes, Shakespeare Centre Library. According to a one-page leaflet in the theatre's archive (*Shakespeare Memorial Theatre: an Account of the Act Drop*, n.d.), the act-drop, first seen when the theatre opened in 1879,

was repaired in 1895, and 'restored and in part repainted' in 1903. Its imaginary scene of Queen Elizabeth on her way to the Globe theatre 'form[ed] a prelude to the plays of Shakespeare as acted upon the stage of the Memorial Theatre'.

11. Electric stage lighting was installed in 1907 (Pringle, p. 22). On film lighting (and the use of purple closed arc lamps), see Low, *The History of the British Film, 1914–1918*, p. 224–5.

12. On paintings on this subject by Millais and others, see Roy Strong, '*And When Did You Last See Your Father?' The Victorian Painter and British History* (London, 1978), p. 119–21. The context of 'classic' film subjects (historical, literary, biblical) in popular culture of the period is discussed by William Uricchio and Roberta E. Pearson, *Reframing Culture: the Case of the Vitagraph Quality Films* (Princeton, New Jersey, 1993).

13. On the stage traditions accumulated by this play, see A. C. Sprague, *Shakespeare and the Actors* (Cambridge, Mass., 1944), and *Shakespeare's Histories: Plays for the Stage* (London, 1964); Scott Colley, *Richard's Himself Again: a Stage History of 'Richard III'* (New York, 1992); and Julie Hankey, ed., *Plays in Performance: 'Richard III'* (Bristol, 1988)

14. Gordon Crosse, 'Shakespeare Plays I Have Seen', MS diary, 21 vols., Birmingham Shakespeare Library, III, p. 96 (subsequently referred to as 'Crosse, *Diaries*').

15. Crosse, *Diaries*, III, p. 92. Reviewing his responses five decades later, in *Shakespearean Playgoing* (London, 1953), Crosse wrote that 'after wiping his sword on his victim's coat [Richard] seized him by the ankles and lugged him out over his shoulder like a sack of coals' (p. 32).

16. Scott Colley quotes from other accounts of Benson's 'mesmerism' in the scene with Lady Anne in *Richard's Himself Again*, p. 147.

17. On the process of filming *Richard III* and the other 'lost' films of Benson's company, as described by Eleanor Elder and Violet Farebrother (Queen Elizabeth), see Trewin, *Benson and the Bensonians*, p. 176–7. See also Roger Manvell, *Shakespeare and the Film* (London, 1971; revised reprint, 1979), p. 19: his informant was 'Mrs. Basil Rathbone'. The hectic procedures of film acting and directing are described in Talbot's *Moving Pictures: How They are Made and Worked*. The cinema needs experienced professional actors from the theatre, 'though at times it demands indescribable patience and perseverance, if not bullying, on the part of the producer to compel the professional to adapt himself to changed conditions and realize the differences between the two phases of the histrionic art' (p. 150).

18. Crosse, *Diaries*, I, p. 35-8 (1893); III, p. 94 (1901).

19. The backcloth of the forum set, dimly perceived, may be that designed by Sir Laurence Alma-Tadema. See Trewin, p. 85–6. Sir Laurence Alma-Tadema had provided some of the designs for an Oxford amateur production in 1889, and Benson seems to have acquired these: see also David Rostron, 'F. R. Benson's Early Productions of the Roman Plays at Stratford-upon-Avon', *Theatre Notebook*, XXV (1970–71), p. 248–54. Trewin's note implies that the *Julius Caesar* production had survived the disastrous fire that destroyed most of the company's stock scenery and costumes in 1900.

20. Lindsey Thomas, in her study of the Memorial's Art Gallery (M.Phil. thesis, Shakespeare Institute, 1999), points out that Brassington made the first photographic record of the collection's contents.

Baz Kershaw

The Theatrical Biosphere and Ecologies of Performance

In what would a postmodern *theatrum mundi*, or 'theatre of the world', consist? In an ironic inversion of the very concept, with the microcosm issuing a unilateral declaration of independence – or of incorporation? Or in a neo-neoplatonic recognition that it is but a cultural construct of an outer world that is itself culturally constructed? In the following article, Baz Kershaw makes connections between the high-imperial Victorian love of glasshouses, which at once created and constrained their 'theatre of nature', and the massive 'nineties ecological experiment of 'Biosphere II' – 'a gigantic glass ark the size of an aircraft hangar situated in the Southern Arizona desert', which embraces all the main types of terrain in the global eco-system. In the Biosphere's ambiguous position between deeply serious scientific experiment and commodified theme park, Kershaw sees an hermetically-sealed system analogous to much contemporary theatre – whose intrinsic opacity is often further blurred by a theorizing no less reductive than that of the obsessive Victorian taxonomists. He offers not answers, but 'meditations' on the problem of creating an ecologically meaningful theatre. Baz Kershaw, currently Professor of Drama at the University of Bristol, originally trained and worked as a design engineer. He has had extensive experience as a director and writer in radical theatre, including productions at the Drury Lane Arts Lab and as co-director of Medium Fair, the first mobile rural community arts group, and of the reminiscence theatre company Fair Old Times. He is the author of *The Politics of Performance: Radical Theatre as Cultural Intervention* (Routledge, 1992) and *The Radical in Performance: Between Brecht and Baudrillard* (Routledge, 1999), and co-author of *Engineers of the Imagination: the Welfare State Handbook* (Methuen, 1990).

1

'All contemporary thought is permeated with the idea of thinking the unthinkable,' said Foucault, and I hope that this article might in some small way live up to his dictum. I say this because it presents not an argument as such, but is more of a meditation on inter-related themes – nature, culture, landscapes, pastorals, greenhouses, wildernesses, anthropocentrism, biospheres.

I think it has to be like this because any effort to create discourse about an ecology of performance will be enmeshed in paradox. How can we write usefully about the natural world from *within* culture? As David Harvey claims, if 'all socio-political projects are ecological projects, then some conception of "nature" and "environment" is omnipresent in everything we do'.[1] So writing about 'nature' will be like trying to trace the outline of the hand writing with the pen used in the writing.

Hence we must be alert to the fact that the act of writing may be reproducing the very pathology it wants to question: the exploitation and degradation of nature by humankind. My trope to keep this methodological problem in a reflexive focus is Biosphere II.

2

Opinion is sharply divided on Biosphere II. 'Living in an artificial biosphere is a noble experiment. . . . Great things will be learned inside Bio2 about our Earth, ourselves, and the uncountable other species we depend on.'[2] Or 'Biosphere II is a monument to scientific hubris . . . a confused tangle of duplicities.'[3]

Biosphere II is, in fact, a gigantic glass ark the size of an aircraft hangar situated in the Southern Arizona desert. Inside at one end is a rain-forest, at the other end a savannah, and in between a coral reef and marshland.

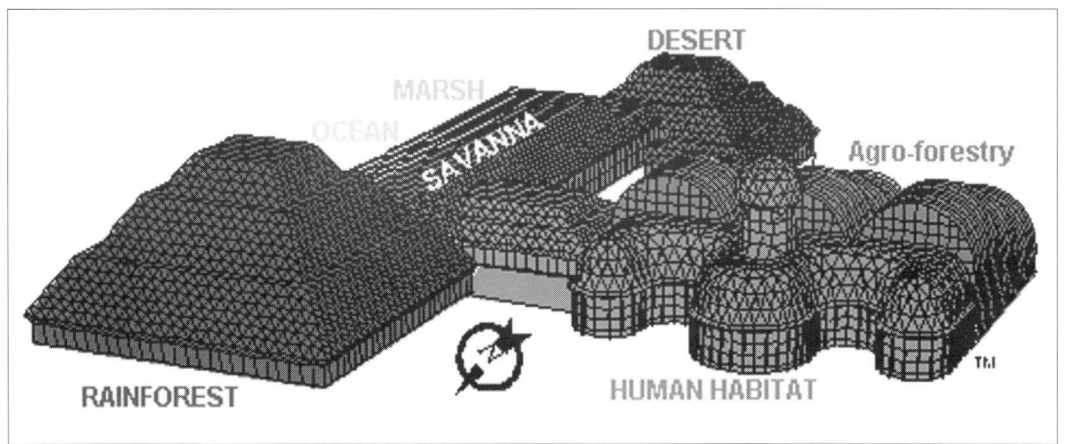

These areas replicate some of the main types of terrain that make up the globe's eco-system, and besides vegetation there are animals inside, domestic and wild – over 3,800 species altogether. Biosphere II was designed to be totally self-sustaining, and can be completely sealed off from Biosphere I – the Earth itself.

In September 1991 eight men and women volunteers walked through its airlocks to begin a two-year ecological experiment that potentially could have profound ramifi-cations for the future of life on the planet. Some accounts claim that these eight were formerly a theatre group. Maybe only actors would have the courage to risk such total immersion in the unreal – or, perhaps better, the hyper-real.[4]

3

In what ways is contemporary theatre a biosphere to human culture? What parallels might be drawn between contemporary theatre and Biosphere II in order to deter-mine the kinds of relevance theatre may have for the ecological crisis?

I am focusing upon *theatre* rather than performance at this stage because theatre is a relatively stable entity/concept, a useful reference point in such highly complex territory. In this article, then, 'theatre' refers to theatre buildings (specially built or converted) and the immediate institutional structures which enable performances to be staged in them. I will return to the question

of an ecology of *performance* later, because my overall purpose is to test in what ways, if any, the idea of the theatrical biosphere might be of use to the generation of ecologies of performance for the future.

4

So if we look metaphorically at contem-porary western theatre as a biospheric ex-periment what might we learn? Recently I went to see Forced Entertainment Theatre Co-operative in a show called *Dirty Work*. The programme for the show says:

Dirty Work imagines a performance as big, as varied, as ugly, and as impossible as the whole world. With an imaginary cast of thousands no event is too complex for it, no human, animal, or geological experience too profound, no gesture too small, no whisper too quiet.[5]

Even allowing for the clear irony in this writing, it is obvious that this show was participating in the pathology of what we might call the inverted *theatrum mundi* of the contemporary postmodern: all the world can be staged through pastiche and parody in the postmodern project.

Two actors are on a reconstruction of a dilapidated proscenium arch stage, a third sits upstage, occasionally playing nostalgic music on a gramophone. The first two actors, dressed formally as if for a night out at the theatre, spend the whole show describing imaginary performances for the stage, with minimal movement and inflection throughout. There was a (no doubt deliberate) paradox in this: here was a foremost company of the British avant-garde ironically, but also obsessively, trying to swallow the very cultural form – the traditional theatre – it had been set up to evade. To me this seemed an irony too far: self-reflexivity disappearing up its own conceit.

But what this saddening show did usefully highlight was the hermetic nature of the object of its attentions. British theatre, in common with theatre in the rest of the western world, is a replica of its cultural environment in a way that closely parallels the 'nature' of Biosphere II in respect of the 'nature' of Biosphere I. That is to say, just as the environment of Biosphere II is 'man made' in ways that Biosphere I isn't, so what we see on the stages of western theatres is 'culturally constructed' in ways that culture in its broadest sense will always exceed.

Paradoxically, this is because the unpredictable complexity of 'nature' – even if only in the form of 'natural' disasters or the dangerous uncertainties introduced into the food chain by genetically modified organisms – is always stretching the bounds of 'culture.' I suggest that western theatre, like Biosphere II, increasingly has been designed to minimize or ultimately to eliminate the impact of such changes on its operations, representing a kind of a retreat from nature. The intense irony of *Dirty Work* was generated by the manifest impossibility of its dream of incorporating the 'whole world' into the 'world' of the theatre that it represented in its onstage design *and* through the company's own place in the British theatre system.

5

So if we view the world, for the moment, as a kind of dialogue between culture and nature, then performance in theatre buildings is placed at two removes, as it were, from nature. From this perspective, an ecological essentialist would agree with the Platonic point that theatre cannot give us access to any truths about 'nature' because it is a copy of a copy. But it is not necessary to assign this kind of ontological privilege to nature in order to grasp the parallels between Biospere II and theatre.

Contemporary theatre contains the 'culture' created by performance like a glass-walled prison, hermetically sealing it off, at least metaphorically, from ecological engagement of any significant kind. This disengagement, I would argue, has been exacerbated in the latter part of the twentieth century by a pathology through which theatre is becoming increasingly commodified as part of the so-called 'cultural industries' of the globalized economy. And this commodification is just the latest stage in a long historical process which has severed theatre from a responsive and responsible relation to nature. An ecological history of theatre in the West, were such a thing to be written, might throw some light on this claim, as the following remarks are intended to show.

6

Una Chaudhuri is one of the two or three theatre theorists working seriously on possible ecologies of theatre and performance. In *Staging Place* she briefly explores the relevance of the history of greenhouses in nineteenth-century Britain to the evolution of the interaction of the human and natural worlds:

The glass-houses that were built at great expense and to enormous public delight constituted a kind of 'theatre of nature', where 'the scientific control of natural processes – the basis of the new industry – was realized with the use of glass, iron and steel in the cultivation of plants'. Partly expressions of the collective European anxiety about the colonial exploitation of the world, partly recognitions of industrialization's transformation of nature into a commodity, these 'museums' displayed the 'masterpieces of nature' to a delighted and increasingly class-diverse audience. . . . Ancestors of the great World Fairs to come . . . as well as of the huge organized amusements of later mass entertainment, the glass houses figured forth a new relation of the human and the natural worlds, making the latter a privileged sign of the superiority of the former.[6]

The colonizing glass-houses of the Crystal Palace, Kew Gardens, and so on, were part of

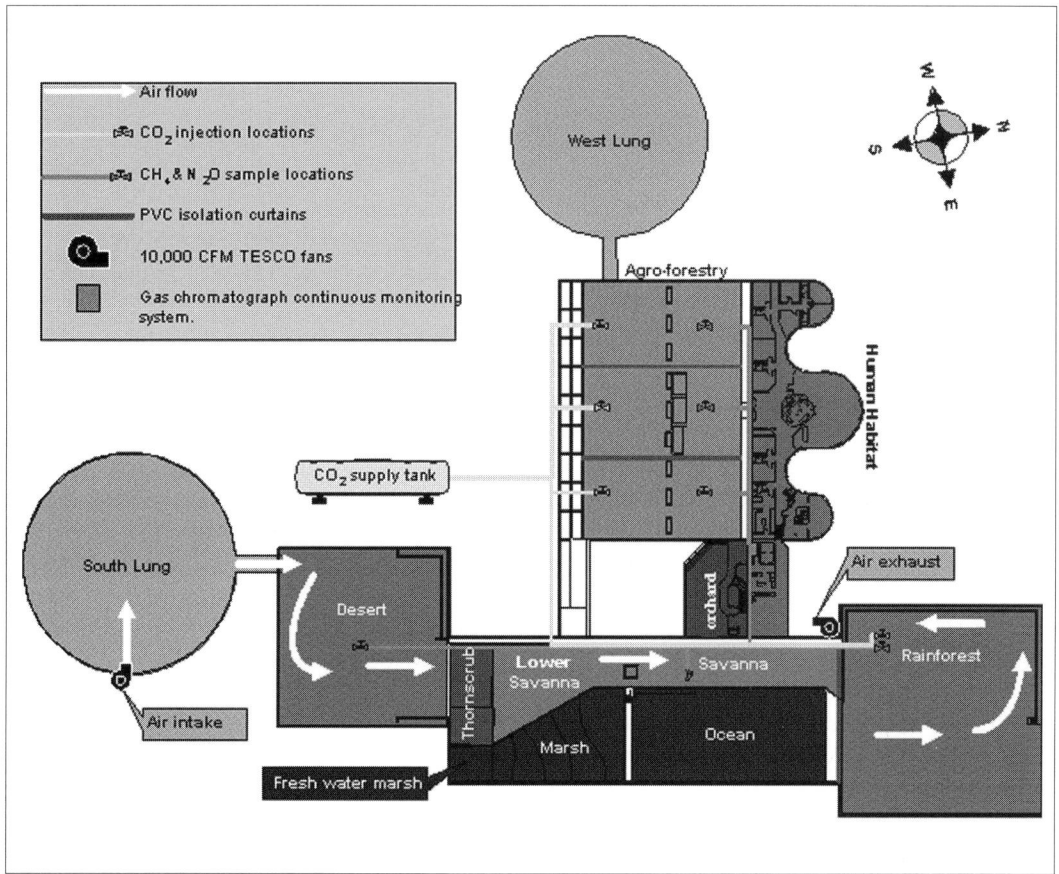

the tradition of Victorian 'Great Exhibitions', which also included, for example, the Empire of India Exhibition of 1895, which in turn incorporated a show in the tradition of military spectacles and 'oriental' fantasies staged at the 6,000-seat Empress Theatre in Earl's Court.[7] Clearly there was a link between glass-houses, great exhibitions, and the spread of spectacle within the picture frame of the proscenium wall in the many new theatres built in Victorian England.[8]

Theatre historians have tended to stress the social and political significance of these shows, particularly focusing on class, gender, and race issues, so that the growth in human domination of nature through the industrial revolution hardly rises even to the status of a sub-theme. We might sense something of this repressed theme returning in the taste for pastoral spectacle enacted by Thomas Greave's dioramic backdrop for Charles Kean's 1856 *A Midsummer Night's Dream* and the other bucolic idealizations hovering in the background of many Victorian productions.[9] But an ecological history of theatre, if we might call it that, which would confirm or challenge such a claim, is still waiting to be written.

7

The botanical experts at London's Kew Garden's were among the chief advisors to the designers of Biosphere II, making a neat historical connection for us between the hubris of the Victorian industrial–colonial nexus and the vaunting ambition of the Biospherians. The Biospherians, though, as we might expect, are very alert to the eco-politics of their project and its implications for the anthropocentrism of the great modernist traditions of western 'civilization'. The people of Biosphere II speak in a single tongue about the human role in the experiment:

Designing a biome is an opportunity to think like God. . . . You go two ways with this. Mimic an analog of a particular environment you find in nature, or invent a synthetic based on many of them. Bio2 is definitely a synthetic ecosystem. But so is California by now. . . . Humans are 'keystone predators' acting as checks of last resort. Populations of plants or animals that outrun their niches can be kept in reasonable range by human 'arbitration'. If the ocotillo shrub takes over, the bionauts will hack it away. You can build synthetic systems as small as you want. But the smaller you make it, the greater role human operators play because they must act out the larger forces of nature beyond the ecological community. The subsidy we get from nature is incredible.[10]

The irony that such 'acting out' – as god, keystone predator, master of the bio-world – can occur only because it is 'subsidized' by the self-same natural forces it has to exploit is not, of course, lost on the Biospherians. Like the directors and actors of postmodern theatre, they are self-reflexively aware that the 'stage' of the Biosphere may be positioned in a deeply ambiguous relation to the world beyond its reach. It is an extremely serious scientific experiment – some have claimed the future of humankind may depend on its success; and it is a massive tourist attraction – with the usual gift shops, cafés, and huge car parks that draw many thousands of visitors to gaze into its green interior every year, as if in yearning for an always already lost world.

8

Part of the Biosphere's paradoxical attraction derives from its combination of transparency (over 95 per cent of its surface is glass) and the fact that it is as close as you can get to an hermetic envelope on that kind of scale: despite its myriad joints it was designed to leak no more than one per cent of its air per century, and it sits on a huge stainless steel tray buried 25 feet below the surface of the desert. It also has two massive 'lungs' which absorb the huge internal pressure of expanding air as the heat rises. I have suggested already that contemporary western theatre shares in this hermetic quality, though I doubt that it is equally transparent.

9

A recent example from Britain can illustrate these points about the general hermeticism and lack of transparency of theatre. Michael Frayn's *Copenhagen* is a play which presents the ethical dilemmas faced by two of the 'fathers' of the nuclear age, Niels Bohr and Werner Heisenberg. Surely a show that deals so directly with the science that led to the making of the atom bomb is engaging, if only indirectly, with some of the greatest environmental questions of our time? Well, the *play* may be doing that, but the *theatres* in which it has been staged – from large regional touring houses through the Royal National Theatre to the West End – are all neutering whatever minimal message it may have about environmental degradation by the simple strategy of its becoming a kind of training ground for the most advanced skills of consumerism: turning theatre – including the live performer – into a commodity, into a piece of cultural capital.

But the theatre aims to disguise its role in this respect: its variety, its spectacle, mask its main purposes, so that its designs on the audience are anything but transparent.[11] And of course the production of capital (partly through, in this case, the creation of docile audiences), and especially the transformation of nature into the commodities of capital, is a key human process in the making of any impending environmental catastrophe.

10

You may go along with this view of the hermetic quality of theatre buildings, but still argue that *performance* in theatre – like Biosphere II – is sufficiently transparent in the ways that it 'reflects' or 'represents' society to by-pass some of the direct effects of commodification on audiences. What contemporary performance deals with seeps out substantially beyond the walls of theatres, thanks in large part to the seriousness with which it is treated in the media, in the careful critical treatment it gains in the academy, and so on. In the main: I think not.

Even if we ignore the negative effects of 'jargonization' created by new critical theory, which has crucially undermined the public role of debate in the arts and humanities, there are few signs that theatre analysis or even performance analysis are managing to develop an adequate account of their objects as part of ecological systems. From an ecological perspective, theatre and performance analysis is always running up against the limits of its own theoretical perspectives and methodological protocols. In theatre semiotics Patrice Pavis's famous questionnaire has a final question which illuminates the potentially disastrous reductiveness in its methodologies: 'What (it says) was not *reducible* to signs and meanings (and why)?'[12]

Seen in the light of the pathology of the great Victorian greenhouses, which would reduce the whole of nature to a system of taxonomies, the limitations of theatre semiotics in the creation of ecologies of performance are deeply worrying. There is more promise perhaps in a phenomenology of theatre as practised by Bert O. States, who confesses with appealing good humour that art, and therefore performance, may always escape the protocols of phenomenology, or any other interpretive approach, because 'to claim [its] felicities of expression as the property of phenomenology would be rather like claiming that a bird was yours because it flew into your feeder'.[13]

11

Of course, I would not pretend to exclude my own work from these reservations, though I would defend it a little, if only on the grounds that it has sought a radical efficacy for performance beyond the architectures of theatre buildings. It is in the practices of performance beyond theatre, I think, that we are most likely to encounter useful components of healthy ecologies of performance.

But even here we must be wary of illusion bred of desperation; so we must test these practices with an especially open eye. Then we might see, for example, that in environmental theatre scenic space is refashioned

mainly to grant both actors and audience greater dominance of the environment; in community theatre that the human collective is ultimately its be-all and end-all; in performance art that the 'nature' of individual identity is the dominant environment; in intercultural performance that it is the betwixt-and-between of peoples at the centre of the barter; in site-specific performance, surprisingly, that it is the human traces on the landscape or in the urban maze that shape the scenario; and that in participatory performance it is the politics of (usually) man-made oppressions under negotiation.

These all-too-brief accounts are infected with a deliberate jaundice, I know; but in the paradoxical territory of the *performative* biosphere – where, say, a wide-eyed focus on man (*sic*) may be always a blind attack on nature – we need to be ever-alert to the potential hubris of every human project which claims to improve our lot.

12

But to finish on some signs of hope I shall briefly discuss the work of three American writers on theatre who have begun to weave a web of possibility that may offer a breakthrough to new kinds of eco-performance. They are Bonnie Marranca, Elinor Fuchs, and Una Chaudhuri. All three have made major contributions to writing about theatre in ways which give due acknowledgement to the complexities of practice, so I offer my comments in a spirit of outright admiration for their ground-breaking works.

13

In *Ecologies of Theater* Bonnie Marranca argues for

a linkage of ecology and aesthetics that in the search for newer and deeper kinds of knowledge [will] outline the biocentric world view . . . a nonhierarchical embrace of the multiplicity of species and languages in a work, that can address the issue of rights in non-sentient being.[14]

She names the Living Theatre, Peter Brook, Grotowski's Polish Laboratory Theatre, the

Théâtre du Soleil, and others as especially relevant to this theme, because they concentrate so fully on space in their work, and because 'surely any elucidation of a theatre ecology begins in the understanding of performance space.'[15]

This follows because, like Gertrude Stein, what Marranca is drawn to most in the analysis of performance are 'concepts of field, space, landscape'. In her writings, though, she seems most taken by the idea of *landscape*, and it is just there that I begin to have reservations about her argument; for has not 'landscape' for centuries been a major trope in the domination of the human over nature? Whether landscape is seen as a source of rejuvenating contemplation (a feast for the eyes of the Enlightenment) or a source of spiritual renewal (succour for the soul of Romanticism), it is always so at the *service*, ultimately, of man (*sic*).

Keith Thomas has shown, in *Man and the Natural World*, how the growth in appreciation of wild natural scenes, particularly in eighteenth-century England, was an anxious reaction to the massive increase in land brought under cultivation: the idealization of 'landscape' was a compensation for (perhaps a necessary) ecological damage.[16] So we should be wary of an ecology of performance that centres on landscape, even in the wonderfully admirable ambition to shape a 'non-hierarchical embrace of the multiplicity of the species'.

14

Elinor Fuchs, in *The Death of Character*, writes less fully about ecological theatre than does Marranca, but she seems to have a more embedded 'take', if I might put it that way, on possible relationships between ecology and aesthetics. Fuchs's central trope for this is the idea of the 'pastoral', because, she says, there has been

in some of the more innovative contemporary theatre an extension of pastoral, or perhaps better said, a pastoral for the age of ecology. . . . [However] there is not yet an ecological movement in theatre. . . . Rather I would say that the new pastoral in theatre draws on a perceptual faculty

not unlike that developed by ecology, a systems awareness that moves sharply away from the ethos of competitive individualism toward a vision of the whole, however defined in any given setting.[17]

'Systems awareness' promisingly suggests something of the complexity of view needed for an adequate ecological grasp in theatre and performance; but Fuchs seems to let it slip in the moment of most acute comprehension when she says:

We are becoming ecologists of theatre. No longer fascinated by single organisms in their habitat . . . we pull back to scan . . . the thing-held-full-in-view-the-whole-time.[18]

The shadow of the trope of 'landscape' hovers over that 'thing-held-full-in-view', just as the developing urban jungle reinforced, again as Keith Thomas explains, an idealizing nostalgic desire for the pastoral in the Europe of the seventeenth and eighteenth centuries.[19] Hence, pastoral may also be a part of the human pathology preventing the much-needed development of an ecological 'systems awareness'.

15

And finally, back to Una Chaudhuri, who has made the most sustained address of the issue of ecology and theatre. Chaudhuri develops a sophisticated analysis of the place of nature in western theatre from the late-nineteenth century to the present. She sees in theatrical naturalism a 'stubborn obstacle' to the development of an ecologically sound theatre. The obstacle is that the environment in naturalism is always 'in the service of a *social* drama', and this is achieved through the turning of nature into a metaphor, which, like the Victorian glasshouses, itself represents 'a new relation of the human and the natural worlds, making the latter a privileged sign of the superiority of the former'.

She also argues that this problem has continued in the works of the contemporary avant-garde that Marranca and Fuchs celebrate, because the avant-garde uses ecology itself as a metaphor. Nonetheless, Chaudhuri is adamant that by making a space on its stage for ongoing acknowledgements of the rupture it participates in – the rupture between nature and culture, forests and books . . . – the theatre can become the site of a much-needed ecological consciousness.[20]

For contemporary theatre to produce this consciousness it needs to make a 'turn towards the literal, a programmatic resistance to the use of nature as metaphor'. But to claim this as a means to create an ecological *theatre* sounds rather odd, because theatre increasingly has produced nothing but metaphor (if it ever did anything else?) especially as it has succumbed to the disciplines of commodification and capital.

This difficulty is not, in fact, produced by any lack of ecological insight on the part of Chaudhuri as she develops her highly reflexive critique of theatre's protocols. Rather, the problem is in the object of her attentions, the theatre itself, which, as I have argued, has *inexorably* become part of the pathology producing the environmental crisis: the transformation of everything, including nature, into commodity.

16

Yet there is a moment in Chaudhuri's argument when, I think, she has a key principle of an ecological aesthetics most fully in her grasp; and that is when she touches on the question of civilization and its roots (*sic*), metonymically signalled through the juxtaposition of books and forests. In the western imaginary which is ultimately the source of the ecological crisis, civilization and the wilderness, culture and nature are locked in a disastrous opposition, with the former feeding uncontrollably off the latter to offset its fears of the abyss – the totally unknown other. Chaudhuri quotes Robert Harrison on Vico to underline the point:

To burn out a clearing in the forest and to claim it as the sacred ground of the family – that, according to Vico, was the original deed of appropriation that first opened the space of civil society. It was the first decisive act, which would lead to the founding of cities, nations, and empire.[21]

It follows that an ecology of performance should somehow play with 'the original deed of appropriation', somehow propose a revision of the separation of culture and nature in global society while acknowledging the extent of the separation. Marranca, Fuchs, and Chaudhuri are all correct in identifying postmodern performance as a possibly productive source for this revision, because it most crucially challenges the dualisms of modernism which have led to the ecological crisis, particularly those between body and mind, analysis and creativity, thought and action.

But clearly, to the extent that postmodern performance in theatre depends on a sustained separation between performer and audience, however ironically framed, then it risks replaying the tropes – of landscape, of pastoral, for example – that reproduce the source of the environmental nightmare in the human.

17

This is why I think that performative events which use an ethically principled immersive participation, transforming audiences into participants, are most likely to lead to new ecological forms of performance. The performative mazes of the Colombian director Enrique Vargas provide, I think, one model for this approach.[22] We might look as well to some of the early happenings staged by the likes of Allan Kaprow and Bruce Lacey; or to the aesthetic antics of protest groups growing out of new social movements in Europe during the last decade.[23]

The immersive experience offered by such events is different in kind to the one promised by the experiment of Biosphere II, or the attenuated thrills of the theatre. The giant glass ark has been seen as a metaphor for human survival against all the odds produced by the human. It is a metaphor which is heightened by the transparent 'act of appropriation' of the hermetic envelope, the disjunction produced by a man-made 'nature' cut off in most crucial respects from nature's 'nature.' Immersive performance events which are articulated directly to what is left of the natural world, unlike performances in theatres, may have the capacity to collapse that disjuncture, to link human nature with nature's nature. They might achieve this in ways that will not reverse the 'first decisive act' that led to civilization, but which could lead us to a fuller appreciation of how we are a wholly integral part of nature. In such small ways might performance contribute to a new ecological sanity.

Acknowledgements

I am grateful to Wallace Heim for drawing my attention to the material from ecological journals used in this article, and for conversations about some of its substance. I am also grateful to Bron Szerzyinski, Claire Waterton, and Robin Grove-White of the Centre for the Study of Environmental Change at Lancaster University for their patience and inspiration.

Notes and References

1. Harvey, David, *Justice, Nature, and the Geography of Difference* (Oxford: Blackwell, 1996), p. 174.

2. Kelly, Kevin, 'Biosphere at One', *Whole Earth*, No. 77 (1992), p. 105.

3. Luke, Timothy W., 'Reproducing Planet Earth: the Hubris of Biosphere 2', *The Ecologist*, XXV, No. 4 (1995), p. 157, 162.

4. Baudrillard has written of Biosphere II: 'A l'image exacte des attractions de Disneyland, Biosphère II n'est pas une expérience, c'est une attraction expérimentale.' See Baudrillard, Jean, 'La Biosphère II', in *Des Mondes Inventés: les Parcs à Thème*, ed. Anne-Marie Eyssartel and Benard Rochette (Paris: Editions de la Villete, 1995), p. 127.

5. Forced Entertainment Theatre Co-operative, programme for *Dirty Work*, 1999.

6. Chaudhuri, Una, *Staging Place: the Geography of Modern Drama* (Ann Arbor: University of Michigan Press, 1977), p. 77; quotations from Kohlmaier, Georg, and Barna von Sartory, *Houses of Glass: a Nineteenth-Century Building Type*, trans. John C. Harvey (Cambridge, Mass.: MIT Press, 1986).

7. Gregory, Breandan, 'Staging British India,' in J. S. Bratton, Richard Allen Cave, Breandran Gregory, Heidi J. Holder, and Michael Pickering, *Acts of Supremacy: the British Empire and the Stage, 1790–1930* (Manchester: Manchester University Press, 1991), p. 151–3.

8. Mackintosh, Iain, *Architecture, Actor, and Audience* (London: Routledge, 1993), p. 35–40. Mackintosh does not make this connection, though his view that gas lighting and the railways were the main technical sources for the spread of spectacle indirectly reinforces the point.

9. Trussler, Simon, *The Cambridge Illustrated History of British Theatre* (Cambridge: Cambridge University Press, 1994), p. 243–4.

10. Kelly, Kevin, 'Biosphere II: an Autonomous World', *Whole Earth*, No. 67 (1990), p. 12.

11. Kershaw, Baz, *The Radical in Performance: Between Brecht and Baudrillard* (London: Routledge, 1999), p. 29–56.

12. Pavis, Patrice, 'Theatre Analysis: Some Questions and a Questionnaire', *New Theatre Quarterly*, I, No. 2 (1985), p. 209 (my emphasis).

13. States, Bert O., 'The Phenomenological Attitude', in *Critical Theory and Performance*, ed. Janelle G. Reinelt and Joseph R. Roach (Ann Arbor: University of Michigan Press, 1987), p. 377.

14. Marranca, Bonnie, *Ecologies of Theater: Essays at the Century Turning* (Baltimore: Johns Hopkins University Press, 1996), p. xvi.

15. Ibid. p. xvii.

16. Thomas, Keith, *Man and the Natural World: Changing Attitudes in England, 1500–1800* (Harmondsworth: Penguin Books, 1984), p. 263–9.

17. Fuchs, Elinor, *The Death of Character: Perspectives on Theater After Modernism* (Bloomington; Indianapolis: University of Indiana Press, 1996), p. 107.

18. Ibid.

19. Thomas, op. cit., p. 243–54.

20. Chaudhuri, op. cit., p. 28.

21. Ibid., p. 29.

22. Kershaw, op. cit., p. 187–216.

23. McKay, George, ed., *DiY Culture: Protest and Party in Nineties Britain* (London: Verso, 1998).

Useful Biosphere II Websites

http://www.columbia.edu/~alt12/Bio/bio2.html
http://www.bio2.edu/

Biosphere Address

Biosphere 2 Center,
32540 S. Biosphere Road,
Oracle, Arizona 85623, USA

Telephone: (520) 896-6400, fax: (520) 896-6471

Barnaby King

The African-Caribbean Identity and the English Stage

In the first of two essays employing academic discourses of cultural exchange to examine the intra-cultural situation in contemporary British society, published in NTQ 61, Barnaby King analyzed the relationship between Asian arts and mainstream arts in Britain on both a professional and a community level. In this second essay he takes a similar approach towards African–Caribbean theatre in Britain, comparing the Black theatre initiatives of the regional theatres with the experiences of theatre workers themselves based in Black communities. He shows how work which relates to a specific 'other' culture has to struggle to get funding, while work which brings Black Arts into a mainstream 'multicultural' programme has fewer problems. In the process, he specifically qualifies the claim that the West Yorkshire Playhouse provides for Black communities as well as many others, while exploring the alternative, community-based projects of 'Culturebox', based in the deprived Chapeltown district of Leeds. Barnaby King is a theatre practitioner based in Leeds, who completed his postgraduate studies at the University of Leeds Workshop Theatre in 1998. He is now working with theatre companies and small-scale venues – currently the Blah Blah Blah company and the Studio Theatre at Leeds Metropolitan University – to develop community participation in

Measured by conventional economic indicators, the African–Caribbean community of Chapeltown is a disadvantaged area – a pocket of poor living conditions on the inner ring of a city which is otherwise riding a wave of prosperity. Yet the area is rich with indigenous artistic talent and simmering with untapped creative potential.[1]

HISTORICALLY, African–Caribbean culture has affected western culture in many ways. Western music has been shaped by Black music, from jazz and blues through to soul and rap, while Black performers play major roles in the contemporary music scene. The influence of Black culture has penetrated many other areas of popular culture, especially that of young people – as Garfield Allen, Black Arts Co-ordinator at the West Yorkshire Playhouse, points out:

I would argue that Black culture is the dominant culture of Britain today. It influences the fashion, the music, everything. . . . Fifteen years ago you could always tell a black guy from the way he dressed; now everybody's wearing the peaked caps, the baggy trousers, the long shirts, the trainers.[2]

This acknowledgement of the major influences of Black culture has been reinforced by the Arts Council's *The Landscape of Fact*, which lists the many areas in which Black arts have contributed to British culture.[3]

Despite these sentiments, however, here I would like to pose the question of how much fair exchange occurs between Black and British culture, especially in regional theatres and communities, and whether the contributions made by Black Arts are reflected in social conditions. Ghettoized communities such as Chapeltown in Leeds show that Black communities are much less integrated than Asian communities into British society. In this essay I would like to look at two major foci of Black Arts work in Leeds – the West Yorkshire Playhouse and the Culturebox project in Chapeltown – to see how the institutions concerned have tried to deal with the problems of Black involvement in the arts, and how this relates to the general funding patterns and YHA initiatives which I outlined in NTQ61.

As a result of the 1989 Arts Council report, *Towards Cultural Diversity*, money was set aside for the provision of Black Arts centres, but after the plan mysteriously fell through

131

in the early 'nineties, the money was ring-fenced, and the Council looked for other ways of investing in the Black Arts infra-structure, the money eventually being used, in 1994, to set up the Regional Black Theatre Initiative. This was intended to improve Black arts programming in the major white institutions by placing Black associate directors and associate producers in regional theatres.

The Regional Black Theatre Initiative

The West Yorkshire Playhouse, one of the few theatres to participate in the scheme, appointed Garfield Allen as its Black Arts Co-ordinator. Unfortunately, over the period Allen has held this post, he has found him-self caught between the white-dominated Playhouse, which sees him as something of a radical, and the Black Arts communities of Leeds, who see him as a traitor to the Black struggle. The causes of this antagonism may, however, shed some light on the different practices which exist and the basic problems which the Black Arts sector faces. Garfield Allen's philosophy is simple:

It's your right to use this building, so I'm going to make sure it's accessible and usable to you, so you can come in here and get what you want out of it, whether you want to hold a meeting or whether you want to get on stage.

Allen's democratic priority is, then, to bring as many Black people into the theatre as possible, and towards this aim he sees three main aspects as his concern: Black work, Black artists, and Black audiences. His first aim was to integrate Black work into the Eurocentric arts programme, so as not only to attract Black audiences, but also to educate white audiences:

One of the unwritten rules of my position is, as an educationalist, I have to develop intellectual arguments to say, you can't judge this work with the same eyes that you look at a piece of Shake-speare, because it's come from a completely dif-ferent location and has a completely different aesthetic. So the first thing to do is understand that aesthetic and judge it on those merits.

This has interesting implications for the relationship between the white audience and a piece of Black theatre at the Playhouse, because I would question whether it is pos-sible to educate white audiences in the aesthetics of Black theatre simply by show-ing them Black plays. Rather than imbuing them with a sense of the *other* aesthetic and world view, I would argue that it is more an exercise in voyeurism of the *other*, serving only to re-inforce the *self*.

Certainly, the existence of such work at the Playhouse enriches the cultural experi-ence of those who regularly visit it, and indeed an impressive range of culturally specific events is available. When asked who this work is aimed at, Allen told me, 'It's an experience: it's for everybody' – meaning those who come to the Playhouse. In this way, we see once again the contribution of Black culture to the artistic life of the domi-nant culture, without much being given in return.

The second area of Allen's work involves trying to nurture up-and-coming Black artists in the area by giving them access to the facilities of the Playhouse. Thus, in 1996 'Art Works' was initiated to fill a perceived gap in training opportunities for Black people:

What is lacking is the essential training oppor-tunities and information networks that would create an infrastructure of skilled artists, techni-cians, and administrators within the region, to place Black Arts on a professional footing and to maximize the Black contribution to British cul-tural life.

The thinking behind 'Art Works' was that while Black people seemed to have been accepted on the stage, there were still barely any Black technicians and administrators. The idea was therefore to give good hands-on practical training, to bring Black people into the theatre, and teach them traditional theatre skills such as lighting and sound operation. Allen's argument is that once these basic skills are taught, the artists are then free to apply them to whatever cultural or political projects they want.

He also cited a new course being set up in partnership with the Leeds Metropolitan

University for Black theatre practitioners, partly to learn production skills, but also to study the aesthetic and cultural background of Black theatre in America, the Caribbean, and Africa. It is a slow process, but once Black people start to be included on theatre production teams or in the BBC, the dynamics will, he argues, gradually change. It seems to me, though, that this initiative is symptomatic of the essential egocentricity of the Playhouse, which exerts its power by attracting Black people within the walls of mainstream European theatre practice. It is hardly surprising that Black artists and communities feel their autonomy being threatened, and therefore marginalized, by what should be an inclusive institution.

The Playhouse in the Community

In a speech entitled 'Where Do We Go from Here?' Garfield Allen proposed what he saw as the ideal structure for the functioning of Black Arts in Britain. This would involve building-based activity in a 'neutral space' (i.e., not the Black communities themselves), and satellite activity in the communities which would be linked to the main centre. But however supportive he may be of work in the community, he is unable in his current role to initiate it, and so is seen by the community as part of the mainstream 'centre', concerned with producing high quality artistic products for largely white audiences.

Part of his work does, however, involve trying to bring Black people into the theatre. The main thrust of this effort has been the 'Upfront Comedy Club', which is a weekly stand-up comedy show with solely Black comics. This has proved extremely popular, but I think it again reflects the tendency of the Playhouse to act as an irresistible magnet to as many people as possible in the surrounding area, a good proportion of whom are Black, in order for certain boxes to be ticked. This may seem a cynical critique, but it is apparently borne out by Allen's words:

The Upfront Comedy Club is a popular piece of work and it sells out every Sunday. I have to fight hard to keep it because aesthetically it's not seen as a sophisticated piece of art, but so what? It gets bums on seats and it gets you an audience in the theatre, who otherwise never come to the theatre. Once they're in the theatre, then you can try to sell them more traditional text-based stuff.

This is also reflected in the attitude of other community work co-ordinated by the Playhouse. Since its opening in 1990, the theatre has run a number of projects – including *Heydays, Playtime, Wype Out,* and *Wyppets* – which have aimed to bring different groups of people into the building to participate in various workshops and artistic activities.[4] The stated aims of these projects vary, but their most important function appears to be 'to give access to what's on at the Playhouse', 'to establish an ongoing relationship with young people', and 'to develop a knowledge and understanding of the Playhouse'.[5]

This is revealing of the self-serving nature of such activities, which are clearly designed as little more than recruiting exercises to build up regular audiences. By setting itself up as a dominant cultural centre – not at all a 'neutral space' – the Playhouse actually weakens its relationship with the Black communities by making them feel excluded and marginalized.

Recently, there have been some more positive community initiatives, including efforts to give support to pre-existent community organizations through the new community network, which now includes over 120 groups throughout Leeds.[6] However, although one would think that a coming together between community initiatives and Black audience initiatives would be very productive, there is surprisingly little cross-over between this area of work and the Black Arts work of Garfield Allen. Different areas of responsibility within the Playhouse appear to be strictly compartmentalized, and a holistic view of community development seems a distant prospect.

One artist who may be considered to some extent representative of the Black communities of Leeds is a community worker called Joe Williams. Between Williams and Garfield Allen there has grown a rift, which is mainly due to basic differences of attitude and commitment to Black Arts practice. From talking to Allen, I felt that there were two things that really motivated his work: a desire to see Black people in all levels of the professional theatre; and a desire to show the average theatregoing audience the merits of non-white expressive work. In other words, his focus is still very much on the mainstream institution and its habitual audience.

An Afrocentric Approach

Joe Williams expresses a starkly contrasting belief behind his work in his essay *What is Black Art?*

Every culture is entitled to see itself as the centre of its own global perspective and still be able to live in peace with all. A people's (re)development is very much linked to their stories – the struggle against the Eurocentric oppression that destroyed African structures are worthy stories within themselves.[7]

This statement reveals an immediacy of political commitment which by the nature of Garfield Allen's post he would be unable to share. It is a commitment to 'Afrocentricity' – that is, the right of a culture to see itself at the centre of its world view. While this includes establishing a peaceful relationship with 'other' cultures, it is primarily about understanding oneself, one's history and culture, and also, most crucially, having the means to express it.

There are three areas within the main practice of Black Arts where Williams identifies particular inequalities. The first is what he terms 'cultural denial through assimilation' – that is, the fact that Black artists can achieve real professional success only if they align themselves with white, British culture. Williams's second complaint is that Black arts events in mainstream venues are often delivered to majority white audiences – which was certainly true of productions such as *A Tainted Dawn* and *Jar the Floor*, which formed part of the Black Theatre Season at the Playhouse. While Garfield Allen does not view this as a problem, Williams believes that Black Arts should be for Black people, as the political agenda becomes devalued in front of a white audience.

Thirdly, Williams is sceptical of the Arts Council's recent encouragement of partnerships between Black and white arts organizations. While cautiously supporting such partnerships, he is aware that previously these 'have always favoured the side with more resources'. If there are to be partnerships, then they must service Black needs, not the needs of the dominant culture, as they have often done in situations of cultural exchange throughout history.

This leads me back to the examination of what constitutes true interculturalism, rather than exploitation of a weaker ethnic group. But I should like first to look at what exactly it is that Joe Williams proposes as his alternative to the Black Arts practices of mainstream institutions.

Leeds Culturebox, the organization run by Joe Williams, is the only ongoing project to take drama to young African–Caribbean people in Leeds. Williams, the only permanent staff member, is paid for ten hours per week, but in reality, living within the Chapeltown community itself, he works three or four times as many hours, and views his work as part of his life and his responsibility as a Black artist. He is committed to the overriding importance of education as a tool of empowerment – in particular, to the teaching of Black history, since until Black people are able to know and confront their own past, they cannot interact on equal terms with non-Black people. He will quote the African saying: 'Until the lions can tell their own stories, tales of hunting will always favour the hunter.'

The three main objectives of the organization are to develop good models of practice, to give young Black people access to these, and to develop resources and a supportive infrastructure. Until now, the work has consisted mainly of sporadic packages of workshops, from just one or two up to sixteen sessions, each package offering different possibilities and outcomes. There have been some one-off or annual projects, such as the Young Asian Women's Summer Schools, run in partnership with Leeds Metropolitan University, to explore issues of culture and identity, and 'Checkpoint', involving work with African–Caribbean under-fourteens from Bradford.

In addition, Culturebox has run a regional networking workshop called 'Two-Cultured' for Black Arts workers to come together and share their various problems and ideas. That these projects have been both small-scale and infrequent has in part been due to a certain amount of resistance from schools, youth clubs, churches, community organizations, arts establishments, and employment services.

Williams puts this down to Culturebox's more controversial attitudes, which are 'challenging the institutions' perceptions of the arts of Black peoples'.[8] Thus, the pattern emerging is similar to that which we saw in the practice of Asian Arts, where certain kinds of practice were favoured by funding agencies over others. Why is it, then, that Culturebox should find itself in the disfavoured category?

The Culturebox Model

As the name suggests, Culturebox aims primarily to allow participants to express their own culture within a closed space, discrete from the influence of *other* cultures. This reflects a very different approach from the celebratory 'multiculturalism' of CHOL and the creative hybridization of which *The Landscape of Fact* speaks. The aim of a Culturebox workshop is:

To create a performance which conveys the uniqueness of our culture in this particular place at this particular point in history in such clear and universal terms that when notated and packaged and received and realized by a group of similar numbers in another place, our culture in all its uniqueness will be appreciated by them and any audience to whom they present it.

Or, as the same document sums it up: 'To know ourselves so well that others may know us too.'[9] A 'culturebox' is thus indeed a box – into which is placed a representation of a culture, which can be accessed by another group somewhere else.

There are a number of stages and exercises recommended in the process of devising a Culturebox performance. In the 'Mental Map'

exercise, the group creates an imaginary circle in the space to represent the geographical area from which the participants come. Individuals then write down on paper things about a place in that area, including what people say about it, a personal connection with it, and a story or myth associated with it. The pieces of paper are then placed within the circle, and participants move round the map to see what other people have written.

They are encouraged to express their feelings about the places, and to see connections, contrasts, agreements, and disagreements between each other's perceptions. A network of connections is thus gradually built up, reflecting the personal experiences of individuals in the group, and finally these experiences are physicalized using tableaux and drawings. While geographical locations are an important starting point in the search for identity, these are really used as jumping points to look at personal stories and experiences associated with those locations. It is through the sharing of stories, and noticing both the similarities and differences between them, that the participants start to develop a sense of their unique identity, not just as individuals but as a group.

Following the use of such exercises to draw out performance material, the structuring of the final product is left open-ended. Williams does not suggest the use of the traditional performance forms of the people involved, since these will often be very alienating to them, but neither does he encourage conformity to western dramatic conventions. Of primary importance is the content of the Culturebox, which should reflect the history and identity of the group. The form should be whatever best enables the content to be expressed, and something with which the participants are familiar and for which they have a sense of ownership. The purpose of the Culturebox approach, then, is to locate the self within a culture and to locate that culture within the world. Communication with 'other' groups is secondary, and will only have meaning if the identity of the self is first expressed.

It seems to me that this rather clinical separation of different groups is dubious in its efficacy. In its attempt to keep cultural identities separate and distinct, the lack of any real human contact between groups could lead to further stereotyping and discriminatory attitudes. But in practice it is difficult to be judgemental, simply because the model has not had enough support to be as yet properly tested. This may hopefully change, since the Culturebox organization has recently proposed a three-year development plan, involving outreach and access workshops, targeted at different groups of people each year, and long-term development projects to create sustainable work with existing groups. There would also be continuing Black Arts networking activity, and a full-time co-ordinator and part-time development worker would be appointed.

Applications have been made to a number of sources for the £70,000 needed, but Williams's own prediction is that the money will not be found, that the three-year plan will effectively be dropped, and that the organization will continue to operate in its current underfunded, understaffed fashion. Despite the existence of some solid working models and highly committed workers, we can clearly see one particular practice – of Black theatre initiatives in regional theatres – being prioritized over culturally specific community regeneration, not because of the relative merits of their practices, but because of an inbuilt bias in the funding system.

Notes and References

1. Garfield Allen, *Activate: the Journal of the West Yorkshire Playhouse Arts Development Unit*, No. 1 (Autumn–Winter 1996), p. 4.

2. Interview with Garfield Allen by the author, 3 March 1998. Unless otherwise attributed, all comments by Garfield Allen are from this source.

3. Garfield Allen, *Activate*, op. cit., p. 14.

4. See *Network: Review of Community and Education Department*, West Yorkshire Playhouse, 1993.

5. Ibid.

6. Information from interview with Maureen Rooksby, 8 January 1998.

7. Joe Williams, *What Is Black Art?*, 1997.

8. Joe Williams, *Leeds Culturebox*, 1997, p. 2.

9. Ibid., p. 1.

Claire Cochrane

Theatre and Urban Space: the Case of Birmingham Rep

In NTQ61, Deborah Saivetz described the attempts over the past decade of the Italian director Pino DiBuduo to create 'invisible cities' – performances intended to restore the relationship between urban spaces and their inhabitants, through exploring the actual and spiritual histories of both. Earlier in the present issue, Baz Kershaw suggests some broader analogies between the theatre and its macrocosmic environment. Here, Claire Cochrane, who teaches at University College, Worcester, narrows the focus to a particular British city and the role over time of a specific theatre in relation to its urban setting. Her subject is the history and development of the Birmingham Repertory Theatre in relation to the city – of which its founder, Barry Jackson, was a lifelong resident – as an outcome of the city's growth in the wake of the Industrial Revolution, which made it distinctive in terms of its manufactures, the workers and entrepreneurs who produced them, and a civic consciousness that was disputed yet also shared. She traces, too, the transition between old and new theatre buildings and spaces which continued to reflect shifting class and cultural relationships as the city, its politicians, and its planners adapted to the second half of the twentieth century.

WE KNOW that theatre is peculiarly dependent on physical space shared simultaneously by the actors (or signs of performance) and the audience. How theatre space is constructed, and where and how it dictates the spatial relationship between performer and watcher, are constantly negotiated and renegotiated. To use Lefebvre's spatial categories, the space of theatre is at once real and ideal space: that is, it is to do with both social practice and mental activity, and it is of course quintessentially a 'producing space'.[1] As a result the performance space is never (*pace* Peter Brook) empty, no matter how bare of concrete objects. How a particular representation of theatre is perceived (and this will determine its artistic, and indeed economic, success) is crucially experienced in space.

Theatre defined as permanently built and specifically designated space enters a much broader zone of social, nearly always urban space, and is thus subject to the contexts and constraints which have produced that urban setting. As with any building, the architecture and location of a theatre building are generally understood by the historian to be the product of a moment in time which is a complex amalgam of artistic, social, economic, and political factors which also determine the wider spatial relations. If historical narrative is spatialized and we 'shake up the normal flow of the linear text to allow other more lateral connections to be made', as Edward Soja recommends, then what is revealed is a map of 'simultaneous relations and meanings' which might enable a more efficacious critique of all the social consequences of enacted ideology.[2] Extrapolating from this for the study of theatre suggests that an analysis of the 'making of geography' illuminates the making of history and the likely contingencies which dictate the sustainability of the theatrical project.

The artistic, social, and political aims of the British repertory theatre movement arose from a pan-European response to the expansion of nation states and the advance of capitalism. The repertory theatres which very gradually emerged in Ireland, England, and Scotland before the First World War were both a product of and a reaction against the economic power which was the basis of Britain's imperial status and colonial control.

Of the problematics which are embedded in the history of the movement one, in the context of this paper, stands out. All the early repertory theatres were founded in major cities – Dublin (1904),[3] Manchester (1908), Glasgow (1909), Liverpool (1911), Birmingham (1913) – but their collective ethos was fundamentally anti-urban. That is, they were positioned in opposition to the perceived effects of urbanization in its industrial manifestation. Just as the theorists of the German School – Max Weber, Georg Simmel, *et al.* – explored an 'ideal-typical condition of the city'[4] which could ameliorate modern urban alienation, so their counterparts in the repertory movement saw theatre as a meaningful intervention in the urban experience.

These theatres were in the city but not of the city, in the sense that the capitalist pressures which drove the urban engine were rejected. Given the way the industrial city had evolved and continued to evolve spatially, there was thus a radical disjunction between the spaces inside and outside the theatre buildings. Now, after the passage of nearly a century, despite all the strategies (some willing, some enforced) deployed by the present network of regional, subsidized theatres to achieve a creative synergy with their urban environment, that disjunction still exists.

Birmingham: Industrial City, Urban Theory

To illustrate my argument, I am going to focus on the Birmingham Repertory Theatre. Birmingham became the second largest city in Britain. Like the Abbey Theatre and the Manchester Gaiety Theatre, Birmingham Rep owed its concrete existence to a private patron. In the case of the Dublin and Manchester projects that patron, Annie Horniman, moved missionary-style out of her native London milieu in search of the objects of her largesse. Barry Jackson, the Rep's patron, was, however, born in Birmingham, built the theatre, acted, directed, and designed in the early years, and, as a manager of national status, remained associated with the city and the theatre throughout his life.

It was in 1935 that the creation of a local Trust released Jackson from financial liability

and effectively committed the theatre to the City of Birmingham, although Jackson himself remained Governing Director until his death in 1961. By that time his theatre was in receipt of both municipal and state revenue funding from Birmingham City Council and from the Arts Council of Great Britain.

When the company was housed in a new building in 1971, moves to rename the new theatre after Jackson were strongly resisted. This was now a civic enterprise substantially maintained by civic money, and this was reflected in its name. The theatre represents the city – or, to use Lefebvre's categories again, the representational space of theatre is part of the representation of space as conceived by the city's governing elite.[5]

However, in common with most urban, building-based, not-for-profit theatres across the UK, Birmingham Rep has never been economically viable without either private or public subsidy. In a city with a population of over one million, ticket sales alone cannot maintain the company or the fabric of the building. So to what extent is the city represented in the theatre?

Birmingham became one of the most important of the new kind of industrial cities to emerge from the British industrial revolution, which made the British nation-state the most heavily industrialized in the world. By 1911 four-fifths of the British population lived in areas which could be defined as urban. The British experience was thus an urban experience, and yet, as the urban sociologist R. E. Pahl pointed out in 1970, basing his comments on the paucity of systematic British urban analysis, the natives seemed singularly reluctant to accept the fact.[6]

Indeed, a subsequent account of the consequences of British urban planning in the post-Second World War period of social reconstruction concludes that 'the professional imagination' of urban planners was 'essentially backward-looking and anti-urban'. There was a failure to address the likely impact of the constant change and unpredictability which characterizes market-driven urban culture, and planners appeared to base their strategy on a paternalistic vision of a 'green and pleasant' feudal village-style city where socially mixed communities replicated the kind of neighbourly relations supposed to prevail in the countryside. Socially mixed did not necessarily mean more equal.[7]

Much the same could be said about the planning of theatre provision in the same period, which essentially set out to expedite schemes formulated in the late nineteenth century. Under the twin influences of late Romanticism and Fabian Socialism, the first repertory experiments were predicated on the belief that effective, reforming theatre could best be achieved through the efforts of relatively small, appropriately educated groups who could then legitimately pass on the responsibility to the state.

Although the early repertory theatres were always financially precarious – by the end of the First World War both Glasgow and Manchester had failed – an important factor at their inception was the support of the local civic establishment. This included wealthy industrialists who had laid the foundations of economic prestige and now wanted to promote cultural capital; academics from the newly established redbrick universities, which were also a product of burgeoning urban status; important members of the professions – and even eminent churchmen, anxious to exploit the socioethical possibilities of theatre. In Birmingham this support proved crucial: at two moments of crisis provoked by poor audiences – in 1924 when Jackson closed the theatre for seven months, and when he contemplated this again in 1934 – prominent members of the influential Civic Society led the rescue campaign.

After the Second World War, and especially in the aftermath of the Local Government Act of 1948, this same sector of urban society was heavily represented on the honorary boards of management which now oversaw the new, not-for profit subsidized theatres along with the local politicians holding the municipal purse strings. Arts Council officers consciously planned in spatial terms to achieve nationwide coverage, often promoting patterns of rural touring out from a central urban base to provide theatre for so-called 'theatreless areas'.[8]

As urban renewal programmes got under way in the late 'fifties and 'sixties, new civic theatres began to appear in major towns and cities, in some cases rising out of the rubble of redevelopment. The physical landscape of British theatre at the end of the century consists of old, refurbished, and new urban buildings, most suffering chronic financial problems. This situation was exacerbated by the first phase of the National Lottery, with its relentless emphasis on capital building projects which then failed to find appropriate revenue funding.

The Changing Face of Urbanization

David Harvey's Marxist analysis of the urbanization of capital explores the way the rise of the industrial city in the nineteenth century meant that the whole basis of urbanization had to shift away from pre-industrial 'mercantilist proclivities and monopolistic practices' towards a much freer flow of capital and labour power. The old assertion of the 'primacy of place' was to give way to the 'capitalist organization of space in which relative rather than absolute locations had to dominate'.[9] Labour is no longer predicated on the needs of social life, but functions independently of that priority in the interests of producing the surpluses which power capitalism.

'The space of power' is Lefebvre's abstract space,[10] but there is nothing abstract about the observable consequences of the urge constantly to change and develop, destroy and recreate. The urban landscape is produced, used, and then discarded in a continuous cycle. Hence the once-thriving areas of the inner-cities decay, while ever-expanding urban boundaries embrace new business and factory developments together with the peripheral estates which house the workforce.

One of the key – indeed well-rehearsed – differences between the pre-industrial and the industrial city is the extent to which the pre-industrial city centres appeared socially integrated. Leaving aside the landed aristocracy who were in a completely different (if in the British context highly significant) spatial category, master and men, rich and poor, lived cheek-by-jowl, packed together in diverse living spaces.[11] Despite the clear socio-spatial differences on the micro-level, on the macro-level these combined to create an homogenous spatial impression. The space of work and the domestic space might well have been the same.

What changed in the industrial era was that the owners of capital contrived to put as much space as possible between their domestic comfort and their working environment. For the much-expanded workforce, living accommodation was typically supplied in close proximity to the mills, factories, mines, docks, etc. But the desirability of space between work and home became an established principle – and, as social mobility for the workforce improved, something to be aspired to.[12] As a result, inter-urban transportation systems developed and expanded with the growing suburbs, giving, as Harvey points out,[13] the spatial illusion of proximity within distance.

The urbanization process saw the mass movement of population not simply from the rural into newly industrial areas but also across national boundaries within the United Kingdom. Enclaves within cities which consciously maintain separate ethnic and national identities were and remain nothing new in urban life. What was now different was the sheer scale of the phenomenon.

Further immigration from Europe caused by political trauma was augmented by the dissolution of the British Empire after the Second World War, which brought both political and economic migrants from the former British colonies in the Caribbean, Asia, and Africa. Birmingham's population, for example, is now nearly a quarter minority ethnic. What Harvey has to say with reference to the way the working class sought a new definition of community 'as part of its own tactic of survival'[14] against the effects of industrial capitalism might well be applied to all urban communities of 'otherness' existing within a potentially alien environment.

What this means is that while cities, like nation-states, seek aggrandisement through expansion and incorporation, the corporate identity, however desirable for economic and political advantage, can never be assured. While it is the business of administrative elites to promulgate the city as a unified, coherent 'subject', the reality is always fragmented and never stable.

If, then, a single theatrical enterprise – in, moreover, a single building – is perceived and maintained by civic and state authorities as representative of the city, then the project must inevitably be problematic. Also of course while the architectural unit of theatre might in appearance seem fixed – frozen even – in time, and dependent on protection from market forces, the spatial relationship to the surrounding environment will be constantly changing.

Entertainment and Community Access

Harvey also points out that under capitalism 'production is typically separated from consumption' by market exchange; and that the spatial division of consumption means that 'vacation, leisure, and entertainment places' are 'separate from spaces of daily reproduction', even on the level of popping out of the office for a sandwich at lunchtime.[15] Even when discrete urban communities consider themselves to be self-sufficient in food, for example, virtually nothing of what is sold has been grown, manufactured, or even collected for sale in the immediate vicinity.

If the basic provision of food and other staples of existence require what is in fact a considerable expenditure of spatial energy, then the need to seek out a source of entertainment must be pressing for an equivalent expenditure. This was recognized in relation to theatre in the 'fifties, when hard economic choices compelled the Arts Council to focus on buildings rather than touring. For a while subsidized transport schemes were developed in order to encourage audiences to travel to theatres becoming more and more confined to city centres. Now, one aspect of end-of-century urban anxiety is the fear of the city centre and lurking danger which acts as a deterrent to the core affluent audiences.

As capital investments, theatre buildings have been subject to economic fluctuations as much as any other industrial unit. The boom in commercial theatre building towards the end of the nineteenth century was in response to the mass-market potential for entertainment as the cities expanded, and improved transportation enabled the middle classes to travel from suburbs to theatres located in central business districts (CBDs) with relative ease. Indeed, performance times tended to be brought forward to accommodate last trains and buses. However, while the galleries and pit benches of the central theatres were filled with the less affluent, the siting of new popular theatres and music halls in the working-class residential areas located on the edge of the CBDs and manufacturing zones could permit a sense of easily accessible community ownership. [16]

When the tidal wave of economically efficient cinemas swept the majority of such peripheral theatres away in the 'twenties and 'thirties, community access to entertainment was, if anything, enhanced, with perhaps two cinemas co-existing happily in an area where there had been but one theatre. Furthermore, the flexible timing of the cinemas was hospitable to workers constrained by rigidly controlled working hours and shift systems.

Commercial theatre producers responded to this challenge with the development of twice-nightly or weekly repertory which – until the arrival of television shifted the site of theatre into the home – offered a viable alternative. The industrial pragmatism of this sector, which seemed to condemn actors to a relentless treadmill of performance, was very consciously demonized by post-1945 arts officers as a pernicious obstacle to artistic development.[17]

The carefully regulated performance times which have remained pretty much standard for all building-based theatre since the demise of twice-nightly rep are predicated on an unexamined assumption of a uniform spatial-temporal working experience which has clear implications of actual social exclusion. Ironically, the dominance of global post-industrial capitalism has meant unpre-cedented temporal pressures exerted on all social groups – but especially on the 'high-powered' executive and professional classes. Furthermore, the spatial division between production and consumption might now be hundreds of miles.

The Birmingham 'Civic Gospel'

No two cities and no two theatres are ever entirely the same. As the urban geographer Tim Hall has pointed out, 'the only consistent thing about cities is that they are always changing'.[18] Both Birmingham Rep buildings appeared at times – in 1913 and 1971 – when the city was undergoing major spatial change. By Act of Parliament, Birmingham tripled its size in 1911, acquiring an additional 30,123 acres of land by incorporating outlying urban and rural districts.[19]

The Birmingham which had developed during the early nineteenth century had not conformed to the stereotype of the industrial city as delineated by creative writers like Charles Dickens – or by Engels, for example, in his description of Manchester. Birmingham's manufacturing strength was based on the processing of a variety of malleable metals, especially brass. Products included 'toys' – i.e., small fancy goods made from metal – mass-produced jewellery, and guns. Typically the industrial plant was a small workshop employing craftsmen rather than a huge factory or mill dependent on a mass of unskilled labour.[20]

An intellectually dynamic, entrepreneurial middle class able to forge a political alliance with their skilled workforce, developed very rapidly.[21] The combination of nonconformist Christianity and radical Liberal politics, as practised by a small, elite group of families untroubled by major class conflict, powered 'a civic gospel' which created what was dubbed in 1890 'the best governed city in the world'.[22]

Harvey points out that the formation of a sound physical and social infrastructure – the provision of clean water, sewage disposal, gas, electricity, education, etc. – was vital to the successful reproduction of both capital and labour power and the maintenance of capitalist hegemony.[23] Indeed, Joseph Chamberlain – the wealthy screw manufacturer and future cabinet minister, who was mayor between 1873 and 1876 – compared the work of a great corporation to 'a joint-stock company, in which the directors are represented by the Councillors of the City'. The dividends were the health, wealth, happiness, and education of the community.[24] But the very poorest still failed to benefit: where slums were cleared in the city centre the goal was to create impressive new civic buildings and a major shopping street. Rehousing the poor was to be left to the uncertainties of private initiative.[25]

There was visible evidence of cultural capital, however, in the monumental Museum and Art Gallery, the Central Reference Library, the School for Jewellers and Silversmiths, and the Municipal School for Art. In 1904 a leading figure in the Arts and Crafts movement, which was flourishing in the city around the turn of the century, described Birmingham as a 'wonderful place: a curious mixture of bourgeoisie and romance, dullness, and intellectual activity; materialism and spirituality'.[26] While Jackson briefly trained as an architect, he also attended the School for Art.

The Origins of Birmingham Rep

It is instructive to trace the early progress of Birmingham's repertory theatre project through the urban space. Like Mrs. Annie Horniman, whose family had become rich from the sale of packeted tea, the Jackson fortune derived from the growing retail food market. George Jackson, Barry Jackson's father, who had begun work as a penniless assistant in a grocer's shop, died in 1906 the proprietor of a chain of stores. The substantial family house and garden where the first performances by Jackson's amateur group were given was located in Moseley, a well-to-do suburb some two miles south-west of the city centre.

The company was publicly launched in 1907 in the dingy mission hall of St Jude's Anglican Church, which served one of the worst of the uncleared slum districts, lying to the east of the central area. But within a year this was abandoned in favour of the Assembly Rooms in Edgbaston – a formerly exclusive area barely a mile south of the centre, which was unusual in that the land was owned and developed in the mid-nineteenth century for high-status housing as an aristocratic speculation. The cream of the city's elite – 'the Council House at home'[27] – lived there, and it was the location for Britain's first redbrick university.

In 1921, Jackson made it clear that he consciously rejected the possibility of cultivating a popular audience. He compared the Rep with the Old Vic, which was then successfully supplying cheap and robust opera and Shakespeare for the working classes of the impoverished inner-London boroughs of Lambeth and Southwark. The 'vigorous colour and action' so beloved by 'this type of audience'[28] derived from the social goals of managers Emma Cons and her niece Lilian Baylis. But the Rep's mission as stated by Jackson in 1924 was artistic not social:

to enlarge and increase the aesthetic sense of the public in the theatre; to give living authors an opportunity of seeing their works performed; and to learn something from revivals of the classics; in short, to serve an art instead of making that art serve a commercial purpose.[29]

Jackson's enterprise required, then, just the kind of intellectually discerning audience which was there in force for the first night in the new theatre in 1913.

Jackson had absolute control over the physical space inside what was Britain's first purpose-built repertory theatre, and as a result he could offer both his audience and his artists a singularly intense experience. Built with a complete disdain for commercial profit, his auditorium held only 464 at a time when many theatres had a capacity of over 2,000. Jackson's stated belief that 'art has no possible relation to money'[30] represented a quite breathtaking dissociation from the basis of his own resources.

The spatial relationship between artists and audience was derived in essence from Wagner's Festspielhaus model, as mediated by the architect Max Littman's designs for a number of German civic theatres. The nearest parallel was Littman's Künstler-theater in Munich, predicated on a festive collaboration in dance-drama between actor and spectator. Where Wagner's fan-shaped auditorium created sight-line problems, so the more pragmatic approach which was imported to Birmingham arranged the audience in two layers of very steeply raked, straight-sided rows. Although the second layer – the gallery – was accessed from a separate entrance, and represented a degree of economic division, it held nearly half the seats. The audience experience was designed to feel like a single sweep. Everyone was focused on the stage.[31] This was, to quote Wagner, 'a place created exclusively for looking, and for looking in the direction in which [the spectator's] seat points'.[32] There was no concession to social display or interaction. The real and the ideal space were locked together.

The Rep and its Urban Environment

Just as there were to be no concessions to commercial imperatives (in the early years little external publicity, no internal advertising, and an austere ambience of plain wood and marble), there was no concession either to the popular attractions of visual spectacle. Jackson's scenographic practice followed Gordon Craig's emphasis on an uncluttered three-dimensional performance space, enhanced by simple scenic suggestion and evocative colour.

The stage was small but adaptable to both modern naturalistic and pre-naturalistic drama – especially Shakespeare, which was an abiding interest. Two doors opened out from the proscenium frame onto a small forestage to enable direct, if controlled, interaction with the audience. For actors, the experience of confronting that steep bank of intently focused faces was both intimidating and intoxicating. For those who engaged with the ethos, the theatre inspired a deep loyalty and pervasive artistic influence which spread out across England and beyond. But as a space of would-be ideological domination it

The original Birmingham Repertory Theatre, shortly after its opening in 1913.

was quite clearly rejected by the bulk of the urban population, free to validate the project through economic choice.[33]

What Jackson could not control was the immediate urban environment. His theatre was, in the true Birmingham sense, an exquisitely crafted toy, conceived and operated by an independent craftsman-entrepreneur. By 1913 not only was the city itself much expanded, but the amalgamation of traditional manufacturing interests and the emergence of new key industries (most importantly cycle and car production) meant much larger and more widespread factory-style premises, new working practices, and entirely altered spatial relations.

The new city boundaries enabled the prospect if not the actual implementation of a ring of 'garden suburbs', where the inner-city poor could be rehoused.[34] In any case, there was now a clear pattern of 'decongestion and decentralization' of the central residential areas, as working opportunities and transport provision were pushing further and further out. Ironically, there was an odd congruence between Jackson's dream and the hopes of housing planners. Both thought in terms of green spaces. The proponents of the garden suburb idea had learnt from German municipal examples,[35] while the ideal space of Jackson's theatre was, like his German models, built in a park.

The suburban garden, once achieved, would draw the urbanite deeper and deeper into the privacy of domestic space, while there was no chance that the new theatre could appropriate open land in the city centre. The Rep was constructed a mere ten minutes walk down from the grand civic buildings which edged Chamberlain Square. However, the narrow frontage of the theatre looked a few feet across an equally narrow street to the smoky back wall of the main city station, and as time went on became almost indistinguishable from the wedged-in collection of nondescript commercial buildings – shops, a small cinema and funeral parlour – which developed around it. The space of power was confined within the theatre, isolated from the appropriated space of actual social practice, but capable in the abstract of major influence.

A Post-Industrial City and the 'New' Rep

The new theatre both as a mental and physical construct was immediately exposed as a site of contradiction and disjunction. It was no longer a toy or indeed the family 'home'/business which it had become by the 'fifties. It was simultaneously a large industrial unit (destined to become larger) and a major civic emblem.[36] The space of performance and performance technology, the administrative space, the space of the audience, and extra-performance recreation space had more than doubled. So, moreover, had the external environment, which by 1971 resonated with significant emptiness.

Who or what did it represent? To what extent was the past inscribed in the present and how would that influence the future?

Most importantly, now that the theatre was fully incorporated not only into the city's representation of space but the space of state-supported theatre practice, what would be the impact of the abstract space generated by wider geo-political and economic forces?

For all the continuing debates which currently surround urban theory, there appears to be consensus that changes in the international economy signalled by global crisis in the early 'seventies have been 'as epochal in their extent and significance' as the transformations wrought by the industrial revolution.[37] The new Birmingham Rep was first conceived in the late 'fifties during a period of economic buoyancy when the importance of the car industry made the city the centre of a major exporting region. Birmingham, along with virtually all the major cities across Britain, had embarked on a wide-ranging transformation of the urban landscape.

In 1971, when the theatre at last opened, the rise in world oil prices which triggered a seismic economic shift was little more than a year away. The prolonged gestation of the theatre was the result of the deep-seated economic weakness which had started to surface nationally from 1966 onwards, exposing the vulnerability of Birmingham's industrial base with its over-dependence on engineering and metal manufacture. Between 1971 and 1981, while the new theatre was struggling to build new audiences at the same time as maintaining a vastly more expensive plant, the residential population of the inner city declined by nearly a fifth. More than two-fifths of the remainder were members of minority ethnic households.[38] The 'dispersing factor' was more attributable to plant closure and job loss than to the lure of the peripheral green sites.

None of the theatres which were built after 1958, when the first new post-war civic theatre opened in Coventry, was immune from chronic economic crisis, but Birmingham Rep had particular problems from the legacy of its past and the immediate urban environment. A full century on from Chamberlain, Birmingham was statistically an 'average' city with a political leadership which was 'cautious, conservative, and suspicious of change of any kind'.[39] A curious tendency to deride the city – 'a place celebrated neither for fashion nor taste'[40] – probably based on its solid nonconformist, determinedly bourgeois ambience, was never far below the surface of national prejudice.

The descendants of the elite families who had built Birmingham and sustained the Rep were still a force to be reckoned with, and drove through the enabling process for the new theatre. But among the hard-pressed local politicians coping with burgeoning social problems, there was little pragmatic will to develop a complementary arts or indeed leisure culture which is necessary if a prestige high-art project is to be viable.

Birmingham's central geographical position, which had advantaged its early industrial development, was another factor. The opening of the M1, the first of the British long-haul motorways, linking Birmingham with London, not only enabled the rapid transfer of goods and enhanced a road-transport dependency but permitted easier access to the dominant metropolitan theatre culture. In Stratford-upon-Avon, just a short drive from Birmingham, the founding in 1960 of the Royal Shakespeare Company, the first of the two national companies to gobble up disproportionate amounts of state funding, was an added attraction. The spatial illusion of proximity within distance made the city easy to escape from for those who had the means.

Theatre in a City of Interchange

In his exploration of contradictory space, Lefebvre discusses the tendency of architects and planners to offer *as an ideology in action*, an empty space . . . a *neutral* medium into which disjointed things, people, and habitats might be introduced . . . incoherence under the banner of coherence'.[41] To look now at aerial photographs of the redeveloped city of Birmingham in the 1970s is to see the visual design exercise in the variety of mass and outline created by the combination of high- and medium-density housing; the tower blocks dotted about open green spaces; the

discrete play areas; the carefully-planted trees.

This scenario of slum clearance is replicated right across Europe; but an extra dimension in Birmingham was the spatial elegance of the road system. What are effectively urban motorways form dynamic linear patterns rising and diving above and below the lived surface of the city and modulating into broad loops and circles which embrace the landscape. On the ground, slum clearances destroyed tightly knit communities, creating more social problems even as basic living standards genuinely improved. The dual carriageways, the inner ring road, flyovers, and pedestrian underpasses threatened to turn the central districts of Birmingham into an atomized, inhuman shrine to the car – but much more fundamentally represented a last desperate strategy of industrial capitalism to carve the city into a massive interchange for the conveyance of surplus goods.

Into this bleak representation of space was inserted the dream of the new theatre – or rather, a convergence of three dreams. After considerable political debate, the chosen site set the theatre well back from Broad Street, the major road which takes traffic out to the prosperous south-western suburbs. This relatively open space had long been earmarked for a new civic centre, which would serve as a monumental continuation of Chamberlain Square and was already the site of some older public buildings.[42]

Thus Jackson's dream of a visually impressive theatre in a park was now made feasible as a product of civic pride. For the locally based architect Graham Winteringham – whose student training had been imbued with Corbusier's *La Ville radieuse* – his vision of modernist concrete, glass, and light would look like a 'jewelled brooch glittering on a plain gown'. Whereas the old theatre had effectively isolated the audience from anything which could distract from the performance event, the glass-fronted new building made the theatre a part of the fabric of the wider community.

The expansive ground-level public foyer was seen as a continuation of the outside pavement, rather like a city arcade. There was to be ample provision of sources of food and drink. The upper public areas would function like 'viewing decks', where the audience could look out across a harmonious juxtaposition of grass and water. Nearly thirty years on it has to be said that Winteringham's exterior design has survived the test of time, especially now that the theatre overlooks a square created to celebrate the city's centenary, and is situated next to the prestigious European-funded International Convention Centre.

The city policy-makers have spent the last ten years trying to undo the social consequences of post-war planning and to create an environment hospitable to wealth generators and artists alike. In 1971 there was an almost total disjunction between the romantic and modernist (if much modified) dream and the wider urban space. There were no resources to complete the civic centre idea for another twenty years, and the new theatre stood in windy, often rubbish-strewn isolation. The lake had shrunk to a tiny artificial pond which commemorated Herbert Manzoni, the city engineer who had been largely responsible for the road scheme. All around there was evidence of the city's derelict industrial past, and a skyline dominated by tower blocks which housed members of communities unlikely to patronise the theatre.

An Icon of a City's Fortunes?

However, the biggest problem which the theatre had to grapple with was the organization of space inside the main auditorium: the relationship between the performance event and the audience. The decision to double the audience capacity committed the directorate to an engagement with the local market economy which was to have long-term implications for programming policy.

The spatial relationship in performance was to stay essentially the same, with a clearly defined 'acting place and enjoying-the-acting-place', as John Harrison, the Rep's artistic director during the planning phase in the early 'sixties, put it. But the urge to achieve a truly democratic experience insisted on the single sweep of seating with no obvious divisions. The result was a fan-shaped auditorium seating 900, which had the sight-line problems avoided in 1913 and which necessitated an exceptionally wide proscenium opening onto an enormous stage. It then provoked a constant stream of critical opprobrium.

What Iain Mackintosh has recently described as 'the functionalist fallacy' of the period[43] – that no seat should be further than 65 feet from the stage – meant that the back row stretched for more than 100 feet, and thus the largest single unit of audience members was furthest away from the stage. The physical shock to audiences and artists who were accustomed to the intense intimacy of the old theatre was profound. Only in the Brum, the studio theatre which opened in October 1972, was small-scale flexibility really possible.

The strategies which successive phases of directorial policy have deployed to overcome the alienating effects of both the internal and external environment belong to another narrative. Outside the theatre, the regeneration schemes which have remade the urban space once again exemplify trends characteristic of the post-industrial global economy. The transformation of former industrial and residential inner-city districts for new recreational and 'gentrification' purposes, which benefit young affluent professionals, together with the erection of high-profile public buildings, contribute to the impression of burgeoning success.

As Tim Hall has pointed out, flagship developments like Birmingham's ICC 'can act as central icons in the apparent transformation of a city's fortune', for which the 'scenographic' qualities are vital. However, Ladywood – one of the poorest wards in the city – lies a mere 200 yards from an icon which cost £180 million.[44] That the Rep now has an expansive glass-fronted, conference-catering extension which reflects its glamorous neighbour is a product of an 'eighties enterprise culture which nearly drowned the theatre in a welter of debt (and damaged the career of John Adams, who had been an innovative artistic director).

Soja, who started me off on my journey though the city where I was born and first went to the theatre, has explained that for Lefebvre 'the urban problematic has become more politically decisive than questions of industrialization and economic growth'.[45] If the living representational space of theatre is to have a future within the confines of an urban building, this problematic has to be addressed. The record of Birmingham Rep, for all its distinctive features, is by no means unique.

Notes and References

1. Henri Lefebvre, *The Production of Space*, trans. Donald Nicholson-Smith (Blackwell, 1991), p. 14–16.

2. Edward W. Soja, *Postmodern Geographies: the Reassertion of Space in Critical Social Theory* (Verso, 1989) p. 1.

3. Dublin, under British jurisdiction at the time the Abbey was established, was distinctive in that it was a pre-industrial capital city of major importance.

4. Richard Sennett, ed., *Classic Essays on the Culture of Cities* (Appleton-Century-Crofts, 1969), p. 5–12.

5. Lefebvre, p. 38–9.

6. R. E. Pahl, *Patterns of Urban Life* (Longman, 1970), p. vii.

7. David Donnison, with Paul Soto, *The Good City: a Study of Urban Development and Policy in Britain* (Heinemann, 1980), p. 6–11.

8. See, especially, Charles Landstone, *Offstage: a Personal Record of the First Twelve Years of Public Funding* (Elek, 1953), p. 103–45.

9. David Harvey, *The Urban Experience* (Blackwell, 1989), p. 28.

10. Lefebvre, p. 49.

11. Robert Fishman, 'Bourgeois Utopias: Visions of Suburbia', in Susan Fainstein and Scott Campbell, eds., *Readings in Urban Theory* (Blackwell, 1996), p. 23–60.

12. Ibid., p. 29–31.

13. Harvey, p. 20.

14. Ibid., p. 31.

15. Ibid., p. 21.

16. Sophie Nield, 'Space and Popular Theatre', in Ros Merkin, ed., *Popular Theatres? Papers for the Popular Theatre Conference, 1994* (John Moores University, 1996), p. 207–19. I have found Nield's article which similarly draws on Lefebvre and Soja, very helpful.

17. An ancillary issue for the historian is that commercial managers who maintained this system but with genuine artistic aspirations have been substantially excluded from the historical record. In Birmingham, the commercial management of the Alexandra Theatre by the Salberg family from 1911 to 1977 included well-supported periods of twice-nightly popular rep. The Alex never achieved the historical status of the Rep. See Derek Salberg, *Ring Down the Curtain: a Fascinating Record of Birmingham Theatres and Contemporary Life through Three Centuries* (Courtney Publications, 1980).

18. Tim Hall, *Urban Geography* (Routledge, 1988), p. 1.

19. Gordon E. Cherry, *Birmingham: a Study in Geography, History, and Planning* (Wiley, 1994), p. 106.

20. Ibid., p. 65.

21. Ibid., p. 75–8.

22. Asa Briggs, *Victorian Cities* (Penguin, 1968), p. 232.

23. Harvey, p. 30–1.

24. Cherry, p. 81.

25. Ibid., p. 95.

26. Alan Crawford, 'The Birmingham Setting: a Curious Mixture of Bourgeoisie and Romance', in Alan Crawford, ed., *By Hammer and Hand: the Arts and Crafts Movement in Birmingham* (Birmingham Museum and Art Gallery, 1984), p. 27–39.

27. Cherry, p. 70.

28. Barry V. Jackson, 'What We Did' (unpublished paper, 1921).

29. Barry V. Jackson, 'Introduction', in Bache Matthews, *A History of the Birmingham Repertory Theatre* (London: Chatto and Windus, 1924), p. xi–xv.

30. Ibid., p. xv.

31. Claire Cochrane, *Shakespeare and the Birmingham Repertory Theatre, 1913–1929* (Society for Theatre Research, 1993), p. 6–7, 44–5. See also Sam N. Cooke, 'The Building', in Matthews, p. 156–62. For more background on Barry Jackson and the work of Birmingham Rep, see also J. C. Trewin, *The Birmingham Repertory Theatre 1913–1963* (Barrie and Rockliff, 1963).

32. Richard Wagner, *Das Buhnenfestspielhaus*, quoted in Nield, p. 209.

33. Nield, p. 214.

34. Cherry, p. 102–5. In 1879 the Cadbury family, who founded Birmingham's famous chocolate factory, began the process of creating a green field factory and housing estate some four miles south-west of the city centre which was to prove very influential in future developments.

35. Cherry, p. 103.

36. Most of the material on the 'new' Birmingham Rep comes from my own forthcoming *The Birmingham Repertory Company 1961–1999*, to be published by the Sir Barry Jackson Trust.

37. Hall, p. 2.

38. Cherry, p. 207.

39. Ibid, p. 198–9.

40. Comment by the daughter of William Hutton, eighteenth-century historian of Birmingham, quoted in Cherry, p. 224.

41. Lefebvre, p. 308.

42. For a less complex, well-illustrated account of much of the foregoing, see Chris Upton, *A History of Birmingham* (Phillimore, 1993), p. 180–214.

43. Iain Mackintosh, *Architecture, Actor, and Audience* (Routledge, 1993), p. 106.

44. Hall, p. 93, 147.

45. Soja, p. 96.

Martin Rohmer

Form as Weapon: the Political Function of Song in Urban Zimbabwean Theatre

In Zimbabwean society, what may not be spoken sometimes becomes acceptable in song – whether to avoid social taboos and enable a wife to complain against her mother-in-law, or in broadening the boundaries of political protest. In this article, Martin Rohmer looks back to the ways in which song enabled forms of protest against forced labour and other aspects of colonial rule – in times of outward compliance as well as of direct struggle – and considers how urban theatre groups in independent Zimbabwe have adapted the tradition to their own, contemporary ends. Martin Rohmer spent almost two years studying Zimbabwean theatre when a research assistant at the University of Bayreuth, and completed his doctorate on *Theatre and Performance in Zimbabwe* at the Humboldt University, Berlin, in 1997. Since then he has been working in the field of cultural management for the Young Artists' Festival in Bayreuth. The present paper was first presented at the Annual Meeting of the African Studies Association in San Francisco in November 1996.

VICTORY, a novel by the Zimbabwean writer George Mujajati which was first published in 1993, ends with the protagonist, an urban destitute called Zuze, getting more or less by chance into a political demonstration:

Zuze suddenly found himself within a crowd. The crowd was just as hungry and angry as the thousands of people within it. The crowd was singing angry war songs. Songs of hunger. Songs of anger. Songs of hopes and crushed hopes.
Mujajati, 1993, p. 117

A few minutes later the crowd's anger turns into active violence, and anarchy sweeps through the capital. Army units are called to stop the looting and the riots. Gunshots can be heard. Some demonstrators are killed by the bullets. Zuze recognizes the person who fired the fatal shots: it is the murderer of his father, a soldier of the former Rhodesian army. 'Absolutely nothing had changed here', remarks Mujajati (1993, p. 118). The phrase, reminiscent of George Orwell, not only comments on this moment of recognition, but reflects the criticism of a number of contemporary Zimbabwean plays.

The quotation which opens this paper provides a clear picture of the continuity of 'song' as a medium in Zimbabwean society.

It also stresses the function of song as a political and cultural weapon, a weapon which is utilized frequently in Zimbabwean theatre.[1] To understand the musical traditions which have influenced the theatre in Zimbabwe, one has to look to the country's history in the specific context of the role of song as a medium of communication in Zimbabwean culture.

Songs have always been a popular form of expression throughout Africa. They are rooted in all strata of society, and stylistic elements – such as *call-and-response*, *repetition*, or *multiple rhythms* – foster participation, which in turn deepens the bonds between people. Thus the songs facilitate identification on a communal and, as during the past decades, on a national level.

Songs as an Expression of Social Change

Songs have traditionally been both *functional* and *political*, in public life as well as in the private sphere, although often a strict dividing line between the two cannot be drawn.[2] Thus it should be kept in mind that even in authoritarian societies songs could come to have oppositional functions. Certainly the primary role of professional praise-singers was to spread the fame of their respective rulers; yet criticism even of important personalities was usually permitted so long as it remained within the frame of the performance.

In the Zimbabwean context, the use of song as a 'cultural weapon' is one of its most significant aspects, a fact which the titles of quite a number of academic publications adequately pay testimony: Paul Berliner's *Political Sentiment in Shona Song and Oral Literature*, George Kahari's *The History of the Shona Protest Song*, John Edmund Kaemmer's *Social Power and Music Change Among the Shona*, and Pongweni's famous book, *Songs that Won the Liberation War*, are among the best-known studies to deal with the functionalism and political effectiveness of musical traditions in Zimbabwe.

In the preface to his book, Alex Pongweni explicitly points to the interrelation between the country's history and the functionalism of its art, in this particular case its music:

Our music has not for a long time been viewed as art for arts sake, and because of our troubled history, may never be. We take a deliberately utilitarian view of art.

Pongweni, 1982, p. 6

Strategies of Reaction

What Pongweni means by 'troubled history' is, of course, the period which began with the arrival of the settlers around 1890, and which ended (or which he hoped had ended) with independence in 1980. Looking at the music of that time from a political point of view, we can identify several strategies of reacting to a changed social environment.

1 *Modification of Existing Traditions*
For instance, there were so-called *work-party songs*, or *nhimbe*, which were performed in rural places during communal work, or in celebrations after the work was done. Urbanization and industrialization in the decades following the first liberation struggle from 1896 to 1897 caused increasing migration and destroyed traditional social structures based on agriculture, subsistence, and the extended family system. It is therefore not surprising that laments or protest songs about *chibharo* – the dreaded forced labour under the whites – replaced the traditional *nhimbe* songs and reflected the new social order.

2 *Recontextualization*
A different way of dealing with musical traditions is their *recontextualization*, where (by and large) the original form is retained, but its use in a new social context brings about a change in function and meaning. In this category we find *war songs* or *hunting songs* from pre-colonial times, which served as a means of resistance during the two liberation wars[3] and which nowadays can be heard at political demonstrations,[4] in the soccer stadium, or on the theatre stage. Another example is the famous hymn 'Nkosi Sikelel'i Africa' – 'God Bless Africa' – which underwent a change in meaning from the religious to the political.[5]

3 *Syncretism*
Syncretism is a third cultural phenomenon which reflects socio-political change, understood in the sense used by South African ethnomusicologist David Coplan as 'the acculturative blending of performance materials and practices from two or more cultural traditions, producing qualitatively new forms' (quoted in Balme, 1995, p. 30).

Most of the famous *chimurenga* songs – the songs of the liberation war – are such hybrid products. Being well known among the population, church songs and hymns were adapted and manipulated.[6] Aggressive, political lyrics were sung to familiar tunes, and western harmonic structures were combined with African rhythms and vernacular languages.

The *chimurenga* songs, which, as a result of their functional character, were marked by a highly flexible *form*, played an important role in the so-called *pungwe* – the term for an all-night, secret gathering between the guerilla fighters and the local population in liberated or semi-liberated areas, where theatrical forms such as sketches, satires about the whites, songs, dances, and storytelling were utilized as a means of conscientization and political propaganda. On the ideological and formal level, the *pungwe* served as a model for the post-independence community theatre movement, insofar as political functionalism and the integration of traditional forms of expression remained of paramount importance.

A Theatre of 'Disillusion and Debate'

On the level of personnel as well as ideology, Zimbabwean community theatre is linked to the well-known *Kamiriithu* experiment in Kenya, where Ngugi wa Thiong'o and others tried to establish a truly popular theatre according to the principles of Paulo Freire and Augusto Boal.[7]

Within the ideology of the *community theatre*, the use of songs, dance, and mime has a twofold role. On the one hand it has been functioning as a political statement of artistic indigenization, as had been called for explicitly in Ngugi wa Thiong'o's *Decolonizing the Mind* (1987). On the other hand, non-verbal forms of expression (songs included) comply with the African aesthetic – i.e., they are expected to provide vibrant entertainment on a pragmatic level.

While it is not surprising that a number of theatrical productions during the 'eighties should have celebrated the new national self-confidence,[8] critical voices also emerged, many of which refrained from demonstrating national pride through theatre altogether, or contrasted it with a sceptical picture of post-colonial society in Zimbabwe by drawing attention to social ills such as corruption, nepotism, reckless capitalism in the face of a socialist state ideology, growing poverty, lack of economic progress, and so on. The best-known published plays in this respect are Musengezi's satire *The Honourable MP* (1984), Cont Mhlanga's *Workshop Negative* (1987–92), Mujajati's *The Wretched Ones* (1989), and Ndlovu's *The Return* (1990).

A type of drama emerged which Jane Plastow considers a typical example of post-colonial theatre in many African countries: a theatre of 'disillusion and debate'. As a result of the Economic Structural Adjustment Programme (ESAP) implemented in Zimbabwe in 1990, which has exacerbated social and political tensions, this type of theatre has gained momentum.

The goodwill which the government once enjoyed, as a result of having led the country to independence long ago, began to fade. And as the gap between the powerless and the powerful continued to widen, songs in Zimbabwean theatre – by voicing collective protest – are once again used as a cultural weapon. I would like to demonstrate this point with two community theatre productions from the (sub-)urban townships.

Having grown out of a karate club at the beginning of the nineteen eighties, the group Amakhosi from Bulawayo, the capital of Matabeleland North province in Southern Zimbabwe, is a typical product of urban popular culture. So far as its artistic and pedagogical work and reputation are concerned, as well as with respect to its financial situation, Amakhosi is the most successful theatre group in Zimbabwe. In its seventeen years of existence the group has developed into an expanding company which experiments with modern media – pop music and film, for example – without neglecting social grass-roots work, including an extensive children's and youth programme.

Amakhosi's play *Dabulap* was first performed in 1992. *Dabulap* is township slang for 'doubling up' – meaning the illegal crossing of the borders to South Africa or Botswana by Zimbabwean people in search of jobs: the so-called border-jumping, which has become a serious problem as a result of growing unemployment in the wake of ESAP. Very many of these illegal labour migrants are caught by the Zimbabwean or South African police, and those who cannot afford the fine are jailed for a few weeks.

The play is about a group of young male street vendors in Bulawayo – street vending being a resort of many Zimbabweans to avoid unemployment. Still, the friends face hard times. As they cannot afford to pay for licences, their profession is illegal. The police crack down on them regularly to confiscate their goods and earnings.

For Xola, who urgently needs money to pay for a necessary operation for his sick child, there is no legal way of making money: he has only the choice between criminal or illegal activities. Unlike his friends, he succeeds in crossing the border at his second attempt, and aquires some wealth by working in South Africa. However, he eventually pays with his life, when he is stabbed to death by robbers in Johannesburg.

The Musical Dramaturgy of Protest

The characters are caught in a vicious circle of ever-returning phases: street vending – police interference – border jumping – police interference – jail – release – street vending. Thus the action returns full circle, and everything starts again. Cont Mhlanga, the group's author and artistic director, calls the language *Ndenglish*, a mixture between English and Ndebele, with occasional slang expressions. As with so many Zimbabwean plays, *Dabulap* combines tragical, comical, and satirical elements.

The predicament of the characters is expressed in a song which, as a prologue, presents the essence of the story, while as a curtain-raiser it also establishes the appropriate atmosphere. With rhythmic exclamations of protest (*Uphi Lumsebenzi* – 'Where are the jobs?'), accompanied by vigorous drumming and whistles, the actors enter the dark stage and line up at the proscenium.

Dramatic suspense is created through the complex interaction between singing, instrumentation, choreography, and lighting. The first of the three musical motifs is combined with a dark forestage and the position of the actors with their back to the audience. By contrast, the stage is flooded with bright light for the two other motifs, while the actors turn and face the spectators. The drum, which is part of a live band on stage, gives the signal for the changes between the single parts of the piece. Tempo, dynamics, the unison of the voices, and a choreography stressing the line lend the song the necessary feeling of aggression.

The *Ndebele* lines are supported by accompanying gestures, these being not only smoothly integrated into the overall movement pattern but also assisting the orientation of those spectators who do not understand the language. *Motif A* expresses general frustration, still without supporting gestures:

Maye, sathwala kanzima.
  ('*Oh! We are facing hard times' – twice.*)
Bakwethu, sathwala kanzima.
  ('*Our people are facing hard times.*')
Zihlobo sathwala kanzima emhlabeni
  ('*Relatives, we are facing hard times on earth.*')

Motif B, in comparison, is more specific in its text, and complemented by a corresponding choreography:

Asilamali, asila msebenzi.
  ('*We have no money and we have no jobs.*'
  This line is supported by the 'money gesture' of rubbing index finger along the thumb, and by hands displayed in a gesture of helplessness.)
Hapana basa, no work, akhula msebenzi.
  ('*No work' in Shona, English, and Ndebele.*)
Siyalamba thina akhula msebenzi.
  ('*We are hungry because there are no jobs' – the hunger being expressed by a touching of stomachs.*)

Motif C at last opens out the real dilemma of the play:

Ngingathi ngithengise, ngiyabotshwa.
  ('*When I try street vending I get arrested.*')
Ngigatshontsha mina, ngiyabotshwa.
  ('*When I try stealing I get arrested.*')
Ngingathi ngiyegoli, ngiyabotshwa.
  ('*When I try border jumping I get arrested.*')
Ngingathi Dabulap, ngiyabotshwa.
  ('*When I go dabulap I get arrested' – 'stealing' here being visualized by a gesture suggesting pickpocketing, and being arrested by a crossing of the wrists.*)

Compared to the political references in parts of the dialogue,[9] the lyrics of the songs often seem rather mild. However, the political function of stage figures articulating protest and 'personal' frustrations through songs should not be underrated, more particularly since music and dance elements – as for instance a line formation or an angry stamping of the feet – often express the aggression which is less apparent in the words.

Moreover, it can be observed in *Dabulap* that songs which seem unpolitical at first become politicized by the context, especially by the preceding or immediately following scenes. This is particularly true for the songs which express the whole range of emotions from joy through sadness to open protest.

A recurring pattern is the confrontation between the street vendors and the police. Thus the vendor's lamenting songs about the degrading and humiliating treatment by the officers or the prison wardens are more than fatalistic statements: they become a general *accusation* against symbols of power, in the same way as the judge or a party youth are openly criticized in other parts of the dialogue.

A Zimbabwean 'Animal Farm'

Repetitive patterns serving as metaphors for lack of social progress can be traced in the work of other theatre companies, too. One of these is an Harare-based group, Chevhu NdeChevhu, which has produced an adaptation of George Orwell's *Animal Farm*, a novel which is on the syllabus of the schools.

The play, *Animal Farm in the Zimbabwean Context*, offers a panorama of the country's history from the arrival of the settlers to the present day. The dramaturgy is not only structured by this journey through the historical development of Rhodesia and Zimbabwe, but becomes, in the title of George Kahari's essay, a theatrical realization of the 'history of the Shona protest song'.

The songs in *Animal Farm in the Zimbabwean Context* thus emphasize their historical role as reactions to new social realities, whether the working songs in the beginning of the play (which mark the era of industrialization and urbanization, forced labour, and cultural alienation), or the *chimurenga* songs which – like the hymn 'Beasts of England' in Orwell's novel – first instigate the rebellion, and later celebrate the victory.

However, Chevhu NdeChevhu do not stop at a theatrical display of national pride, but set this in the second part of the production against a satirical view of contemporary Zimbabwe. Pompous verbosity in a parliamentary scene and exploitative labour conditions are presented, the latter through working songs and mimes almost identical with those of the first part, where they reflect experiences of the colonial system of forced labour, suggesting that history repeats itself.

In this particular case, the target of the satirical attack is a government programme called 'Food for Work', which had been implemented in 1992 but been taken over by the Grain Loan Scheme two years later. As the name suggests, the workers who participated in the 'Food for Work' programme were not paid in cash, but received food. The group suggests that there is no difference between colonial forced labour, or *chibharo*, and this post-independence, indigenous programme, except for the change of words. The production claims that in the face of growing poverty and the absence of alternatives, the workers of today are forced economically to work under the same exploitative conditions.

These are but two examples of how the traditional medium of song is utilized in an outspokenly critical and emancipated manner in contemporary Zimbabwean theatre. In so doing, theatre troupes have the same options as outlined above: They can adapt, modify, or manipulate them, and thus alter their original function, or they can write new songs. Like most groups, Amakhosi and Chevhu NdeChevhu are pragmatic in this respect, and utilize both of these strategies as seems appropriate.

If Zimbabwean theatrical personnel have demonstrated flexibility and creativity in their appropriation and use of their rich musical traditions, then the general political significance inherent in these forms has been sustained down to the present day.

Notes

1. In her article on Chile, Jan Fairley (1989) has demonstrated lucidly how songs worked as a 'cultural weapon' against the dictatorship of Pinochet. Also exemplary is the case of South Africa, where songs have always played an important role in the anti-apartheid struggle. Songs performed at funerals of apartheid victims, for instance, often led to political demonstrations and riots.

2. George Kahari (1981) describes a situation where a woman makes her domestic problems a public issue.

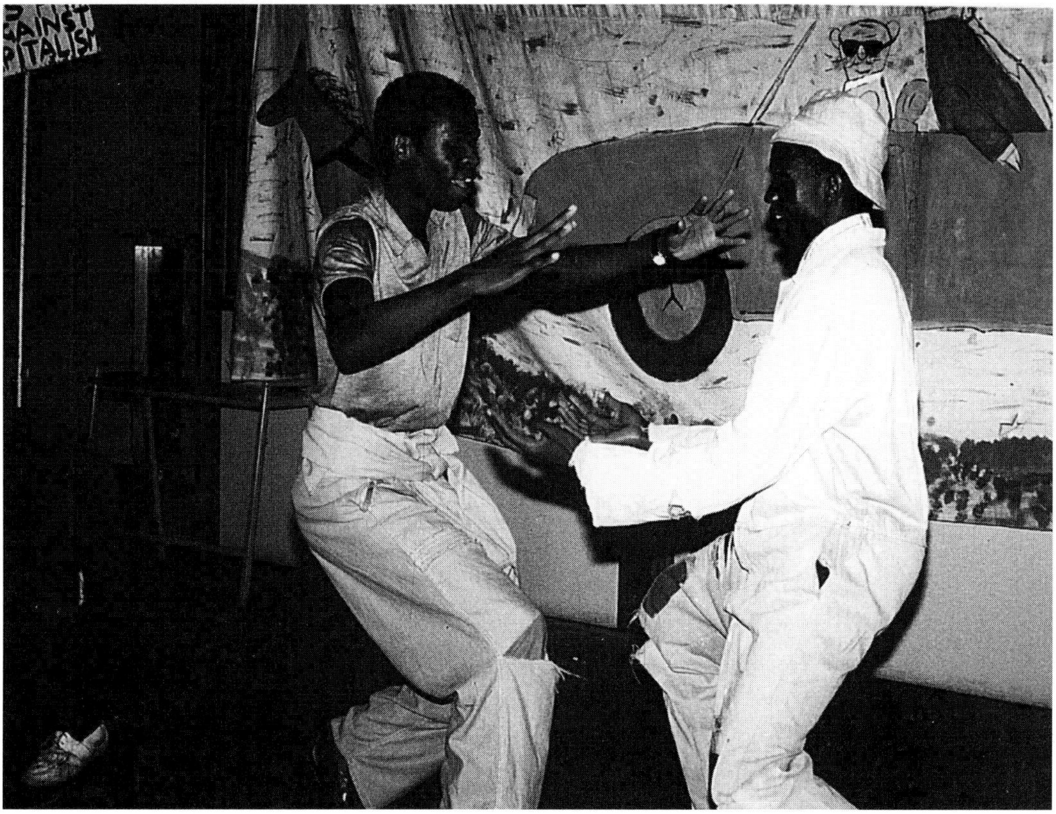

Scenes from *Animal Farm in the Zimbabwean Context*, performed by the group Chevhu NdeChevhu, 1993.
Top: guerillas singing a war song. Bottom: a mimed assembly line of workers building a dam

Criticizing her abusive mother-in-law verbally would be taboo; therefore she makes an ultimate attempt by voicing her protest through a song, a step which is legitimized by her community. Kahari describes this strategy as 'a public but final appeal to the community to come to her rescue in this hour of desperation'.

3. On the song 'Yave nyama yekugocha'('It is meat to roast'), see Berliner, 1977, p. 8.

4. See the quotation from Mujajati's novel, above.

5. It was composed by the South African Enoch Sontonga by the end of the last century. During the 'fifties, the hymn was in the service of African nationalist movements and became a protest song. At times banned by the then Rhodesian government, it later became the official national anthem of Zimbabwe and Zambia. Today, Zimbabwe has adopted a new national anthem. See also Berliner, 1977, p. 20–1; Kaemmer, 1989, p. 38; Kahari, 1981, p. 93.

6. See Sherman, 1980, p . 83.

7. After the clamp-down on Kamiriithu by Arap Moi's government in 1982, Ngugi wa Mirii, Kimani Gecau, and Micere Mugo, who were all involved in the project, chose Zimbabwe as their place of exile and helped to establish a community theatre in this country. Whether or not (or to what extent) the community theatre in Zimbabwe really follows the objectives of Kamiriithu cannot be discussed here.

8. For instance, *Mbuya Nehanda – Mweya Werusununguko,* by the National Dance Company on the first anniversary of independence in 1981; Zambuko/Izibuko's *Katshaa* (1988); and performances of all genres on the occasion of national holidays.

9. See, for instance, Killiam Chigerwe in *The Daily Gazette,* 18 May 1993, p. 11: 'This play is very subversive. Many political issues dealt with at length are too direct, for instance references to the naming of streets as a political ambition. . . . These things are a direct insult to the ruling party. I therefore suggest that if the group is to progress without political intervention, it ought to modify some of these direct political attacks.'

References

Christopher Balme: *Theater im postkolonialen Zeitalter: Studien zum Theatersynkretismus im englischsprachigen Raum* (Tübingen: Nax Niemeyer Verlag, 1995), p. 30.

Paul Berliner, 'Political Sentiment in Shona Song and Oral Literature', *Essays in Arts and Sciences,* VI, No. 1 (March 1977), p. 1–29.

Leslie Bessant: 'Songs of Chiweshe and Songs of Zimbabwe', *African Affairs,* XC, No. 370 (January 1994), p. 43–73.

Jan Fairley, 'Analyzing a Performance: Narrative and Ideology in Concerts by Karaxú', *Popular Music,* VIII, No. 1 (January 1989), p. 1–30.

John Edmund Kaemmer, 'Social Power and Music Change the Shona', *Ethnomusicology,* XXXIII, No. 1 (Winter 1989), p. 31–45.

George P. Kahari, 'The History of the Shona Protest Song: a Preliminary Study', *Zambezia: the Journal of the University of Zimbabwe,* IX, No. 2 (1981), p. 79–101.

Cont Mdladla Mhlanga, *Workshop Negative: a Play* (Harare: College Press, 1992).

George Mujajati, *The Wretched Ones: a Play* (Harare: Longman Zimbabwe, 1992).

——, *The Rain of my Blood: a Play* (Gweru: Mambo Press, 1991).

——, *Victory: a Novel* (Harare: College Press, 1993).

Gonzo H. Musengezi, *The Honourable MP: a Play* (Gweru: Mambo Press, 1984, reprinted 1990).

T. P. Ndlovu, *The Return: a Play* (Gweru: Mambo Press, 1990).

Jane Plastow, *African Theatre and Politics: the Evolution of Theatre in Ethiopia, Tanzania, and Zimbabwe. A Comparative Study* (Amsterdam; Atlanta: Rodopi, 1996).

Alex J. C. Pongweni, *Songs that Won the Liberation War* (Harare: College Press, 1982).

Jessica Sherman, 'Songs of . the Chimurenga', *Africa Perspective,* No. 16 (Winter 1980), p.80–8.

Ngugi wa Thiong'o, *Decolonizing the Mind: the Politics of Language in African Literature* (Harare: Zimbabwe Publishing House, 1987).

Carolee Schneemann
interviewed by Alison Oddey

Aphrodite Speaks: on the Recent Performance Art of Carolee Schneemann

The work of Carolee Schneemann, who celebrated her sixtieth birthday last year, has from the first challenged suppressive sexual and other taboos, and placed her own body as an artist into a fluent relationship with her art. She both pioneered and in her new work continues to energize forms of what we now call performance art. The retrospective of her works from 1963 to 1996, recently seen at the New Museum of Contemporary Art, New York, affirmed her recognition as a major artist – yet threatened also to 'fix' her art, which remains very much 'in progress'. The exhibition included the installation *Mortal Coils* (1993–94), in which a slide projection system is combined with motorized ropes, flour, and sand to explore taboos of death and loss; *Up to and Including Her Limits* (1979), a video installation depicting the actions which produced surrounding wall drawings; and *Video Rocks* (1989), in which a hundred hand-sculptured rocks merge into a wall of seven monitors on which feet walk back and forth over virtual rocks. *Vulva's Morphia* (1995), a colour grid of photographs with text and motorized components, was exhibited at the Pompidou Centre in 1995, and her multi-media installation *Known/Unknown – Plague Column* (1996), was seen in New York and Montreal in 1996. Schneemann's published books include *Parts of a Body: House Book* (1972); *Cézanne, She Was a Great Painter* (1976); *ABC: We Print Anything – in the Cards* (1977); *Video Burn* (1992); and *More Than Meat Joy: Performance Works and Selected Writings* (1997). Her *Body Politics: Notes and Essays of Carolee Schneemann* is forthcoming from MIT Press, and a selection of her letters from Johns Hopkins University Press. Alison Oddey, Professor of Drama at Loughborough University, interviewed Carolee Schneemann on 29 August 1997 in her Manhattan loft in New York, and what follows is an edited version of that interview, which focuses on her more recent performative work.

IT SEEMS TO ME *that the root, the basis of all your work is activating your materials as a painter. What I'm particularly interested in is your recent and current performative works, including installations.*

The recent work is connected to work from the 1960s when I first arrived out of university in New York. Whatever I do that is considered installation or performative is begun as an extension of the principles of Abstract Expressionism carried into actual time and lived action. The performative works of the 1960s to 1980s eclipsed the basic works, which have always been objects and installations. What I'm doing now is building a wall of permutated drawings. They're watercolours in brush and feathers – another morphology of vulvic form. I've been permutating such basic forms in various ways for the past ten years. This circle has gone into an installation of three hundred rounded, hand-made, hand-poured, shaped rocks that then recede into a bank of monitors, in which you see feet virtually walking on these rocks. *Video Rocks* (1987–88) explores the virtual and the actual, as well as the displacement of tactility. *Mortal Coils* – the installation for dead friends – developed for two years from 1994 to 1996. This month I've had to rebuild the configuration of this loft as it was in 1963 for *Eye Body*, with all the painting constructions and motorized sculptures – those physicalized sculptural elements which invited and provoked the integration of my own body as part of my materials in 1963.

This has been an ordeal – to find all the work and materials. Once it was set up here in the original space, it was wonderful and fun. I remembered where I would have had a jar that spilled, a certain leakage over my paint table. I had to re-create certain instant patinas of time, so in a way I was performing a history. I was reliving it, I was performing it, and this makes sense to me in terms of my life and my work being continually interwoven – I can't separate my sense of grasping a past, lived event from how it becomes transposed into the present.

What is the reason for re-creating this work?

A historic exhibit – 'Out of Actions: Between Performance and the Object 1949–79' – at the Museum of Contemporary Art in Los Angeles.[1] It's a vitalized history of how visual artists activated space and evolved what we now call performance or performative forms. To the painters who originated environments and the actions within them in the 1960s and the late 1950s, such words would have been despised. The installation, the actual studio as it was in 1963, will be in the museum: the walls, the floor, the entire surround, and the actual painting constructions in which I transform my body and combine it with the materials of these painting constructions.

These actions were made for a photographic essay with a 35mm camera. The camera speed was very important so that I was consumed by the implications of the materials of the body combined with the swiftness of camera exposure. I couldn't ever imagine posing – which has always been an issue for me. My work is always premised on self-loss, developing a site of actions in which risk, spontaneity, and unexpected integrations can happen. My position with my material has always been to make a situation where the outcome is not predetermined.

So with *Eye Body* – these 36 transformative actions became a set of photographs to capture fleeting imagery. I was working with a close friend on camera (the Icelandic–French painter Erro). Subsequently, I'll be working the camera myself, not always, but in many actions before the camera. I'll be working with a cable release and risking the energy of what's happening in that space with some sense of connection to where the lens is focused. That's what I want to let happen.

So as of now you don't feel a need to collaborate with someone else to re-create Eye Body?

No. I've been completely on my own for economic reasons. People don't spontaneously have time or energy to collaborate now. If I wanted some kind of technical collaboration, I would need funds, and there are no funds to do that. The other thing I'm working on this week is a book for MIT Press. I'm editing five years of my lectures and essays, which is completely consuming.

Is the fact that you can turn your hand to a diverse number of projects (such as painting, film or video making, writing, performing) the reason for lack of recognition? Culture only accepts one label doesn't it?

It's interesting, though, because it's made a mythic kind of haze around whatever it is I do. People feel they might have glimpsed some part of it. In a culture that is increasingly saturated with developments around the issues that I pioneered, it gets even more confusing for people to see whether this was innovative work or whether it resembles something that they've subsequently been influenced by.

Is there going to be any other ongoing work?

I'm going to be performing *Vulva's Morphia or Ask the Goddess* in Denmark in October.

Is this related to the performance of Vulva's School *that you gave in Vancouver in 1995?*

There were two versions of that. The Vancouver version was more of a lecture. It also exists in a performative form. The audience are given cards in advance in which they can ask any question they choose to Vulva. They can ask Vulva anything they've ever wanted to know. Usually, the questions are very penetrating, as Vulva would wish, and often difficult or disturbing. The risks are enormous. I'm usually frightened before I do it: my knees get weak, I feel anxious and disturbed, and I have to remind myself it's because a shamanistic position is establishing itself, pushing against the normative. It's groping towards areas that are dangerous to the culture. I feel extremely naked and exposed in the position of the speaking Vulva, because she represents such a contested territory of taboo energies, genitalized sexuality as a source of wisdom and expressivity in exchange with an anonymous public.

Once doing the work, I've been able to satisfy several contradictory needs. One is to form a didactic base. Visual information is encoded by the slides that are to be projected, without my being able to anticipate the questions. There is a slide sequence that is predetermined, which I use as a kind of tarot set. Assistants gather the questions – reality figures who occur through most of my performance work. There are always adjuncts who keep time or who know where props or materials are – aware of these real things when I'm lost in my work process.

I'll have two assistants, someone on sound with a group of tapes that they can randomly cut in or cut out. I have a lot of props, and also a set of cards that are mixed with the questions that will give me the instructions to do disjunctive actions. So I am in a constant state of tension between being told by my own cards that I have to pour red jello all over my face, or take a hammer and nails and make a three-second shape from the nails. In between, the next question is presented to me by one of the 'reality' figures, then read back to the audience into a microphone as I listen attentively.

'What shall I do about premature ejaculation?' I turn around, look at the slides. Let's say it's the two rutting pigs configuration, so the answer coming from those images on the slides could be: 'To do more, to dig further, to keep going with your animal.' I had a question once: 'My grandfather abused me, how can I come back to my body?' With that question two slides were randomly juxtaposed: a Victorian postcard of a false crucifixion image of a woman on a cross with cropped hair, who is naked except for a rope around her waist – a popular Victorian postcard titled 'Isis'; and a Veronese painting of the Crucifixion. With this configuration I would talk about patriarchal suppressions and the disruption to integral female energy.

But I never know. It's rich, full, and complex, so I can work with this self-loss, where I don't know what I'm doing but I'm calling on my deepest reserves. There are card instructions to physicalize my position, so I'm not just speaking and the interaction with the audience is very intense. It's poignant, it's funny, because my instructions are calculated randomly to make my position as extreme as possible.

Preceding the performance of *Vulva's Morphia*, there is a photographic version of *Vulva's Morphia* with text. A series of twelve statements underline twelve rows of permutated vulvic images that include paleolithic inscribed vulvas as well as my own body. The last statement is 'Vulva learns to ask, "Is this good for Vulva?"' So my questions all come from having to figure out why so many forces, forms, and conventions want to stifle my pleasure, my power.

I'm reminded of an interview [2] where you said that you don't choose to perform, but it comes upon you and you've got to action it.

There are areas of imagining that I can only position by putting myself physically in the middle of the idea. I have to inhabit that imagery and its potentiality. However, I won't perform in New York City.

Why not?

It's too saturated. It's so saturated with my own history and with new forms that they crowd my sense of uncertainty and adventure. And everything has got crazily expensive and over-produced. So I prefer to do a performance somewhere in Canada, or in smaller cities, just where it's unexpected for me. That's where I suddenly start having amazing ideas. I was just in a monastery in Winnipeg, which is now an arts centre. I was in residency in a monk's room for a week, able to concentrate on my writing – and of course, being in a monastery in a monk's small room produced the most coherent sacrilegious insights. It was very satisfying and I got a lot done.

Has that experience inspired you, whether it be painting or performance: has it fed into anything?

Yes. Anonymous and unselfconscious places often do just feel freer, and it helps me to be in a place where I think people don't have specific expectations of me. It's increasingly hard to encounter my own mythology.

Going back to not wanting to perform in New York, I wondered what your thoughts were on the state of performance art in New York at the moment. How do you perceive the scene?

It's certainly a monster we spawned. Happenings, environments, events – those were the generative forms in the late 1950s and early 1960s. With no exception, all this complexity and inter-cutting was initiated by painters – it was a visionary theatre of painters. It was not confessional, never narrative, and there was no idea that it would be absorbed by the larger culture.

The aims and the unconscious directives in much performance art now have to do with the development of mass culture. At the same time there is this slippage where the most difficult, visionary, rigorous sources of explorations are not driving the vocabulary of performance art as I see it now. The need to establish an audience and to have a predictive audience, that's probably important because you can't get a space without paying rent on it. Economics are deeply involved. Many aspects of performance art have gone into mass culture forms (MTV), certain jokes, tricks, gender issues, Hollywood films losing that painterly, art-historical, visionary position – it's doing something else.

Sometimes, I feel very confirmed by the new directions – for instance, Karen Finley's visionary lost shrieking consciousness, the kind of Cassandra warning, the sheep and the wolves that are clawing at our cages. Or Holly Hughes, who takes the denied, suppressed, lived experience of an adventurous young woman who is gay out of the heartland of Americana, or Linda Montano's *Life as an Art Practice*. Most of the forms through the 1970s were taken by women because they hadn't already been inhabited by male structures and definitions. It's very rich, it's

complex, and the body as 'a source of knowledge' which I had to fight for singularly in the 1960s is everybody's and everywhere now.

This goes back to your clear feeling of lack of acknowledgement that you obviously have been a huge influence and a pioneer.

I was constantly giving people permission to see and to look at work which was real in their lived lives, to break through the grandiose mythologizing of traditional male culture.

Are you pioneering now?

Sure, I am. There is always something to fight for. I've finally got cats in the right place. And I've got heterosexuality and its pleasures in a pretty good position. I've got all these issues of genital sexuality, of the cunt, of the speaking vulva – those are in discussion. As well as the denied atrocities of Vietnam, the suppression of Palestinian culture, and now the physical destruction of the Balkans as my subject. Psychic phenomena, permission to work with the unconscious and the unknown. I'm very interested in the fact that I was always lied to about what would happen to me when I got older, that everything they said *didn't* happen.

'They' as in the culture?

Yes – that I would shrivel, have hot flushes, and that my vagina would dry up, that everything that had defined my erotic experience would be taken from me. It's completely wrong.

Isn't that also to do with the representation of received images of the older woman as a non-sexual being?

We have a very narrow threshold of heterosexual acceptability, and when you leave that idealized femme threshold in the popular male cultural imagination, you really are a figure that is despicable, to be despised. You're the witch, or the mother. You don't fuck the witch or the mother. If you don't want to fuck it then, in this culture, they become contemptible. I'm always going to go out there and risk it all again!

Is there still vulnerability about your work, despite having had an extraordinary career in the context of New York?

Yes, always. You never know if you are really okay or good enough. I'm still so confused about what people think about the work or that it matters. I walk into a gallery and think, 'Didn't I already do this?' It's really important that I live in the woods. I've always lived there. It was also a secret. I share this city loft and I just go up and down on the bus, and have a private life there. I've done all the embroiled New York activity and had an amazing community to work with initially. Everyone has grown up and distinguished themselves in their various ways, and this pulls you apart in time and event – Judson Dance Theater, Avant-Garde Theater, Fluxus, Happenings.

And yet, reading the various reviews of your exhibition, 'Carolee Schneemann: up to and Including Her Limits' at the New Museum of Contemporary Art,[3] they almost all began with the aspect of neglect.

It's true. There were reverential reviewers, the museum had 11,000 visitors. It was the first exhibit curated by Dan Cameron, so he had to work within certain pre-existing constraints. There were three other installations in the back, and I desperately needed the space. I'm still not connected to a gallery that has strong museum affiliations, or collectors that are proportionate to the importance of this work, if it is really important. My house is falling apart; I don't have health insurance; I can't pay for a regular assistant – even after this major exhibit, and even after these fifteen remarkable, passionate reviews, which are all so deeply knowledgeable and culturally coherent. As you say, they almost all start with the aspect of neglect, and it hasn't changed. Louise Bourgeois never stopped when she was neglected or when she was celebrated. Woolf never stopped with all her struggles against rigidity and rejection, but also that's an example where we don't have to commit suicide any more, or drown, or take poison, or disappear. The hardiness of the woman artist is inspiring.

So there's a future for solo women performance artists?

Yes, there will always be a future for them in some form, because they are also bringing forward the suppressed forms of the imagination, of the latency of the culture, in solo performance – comics, jugglers, lion-tamers, anyone who can take the cultural unconscious and position themselves in it. There are stories that have to be re-examined and the telling of the stories is going to find its energy, its fertility, in the people who are able to enact them. I don't think the singular acting, moving, or speaking presence will ever leave us. The younger women have no problem whatsoever, because there is now a kind of Dante-esque procedural way that things happen. You are a young adventurous artist and a dealer wants a younger sexy artist, because they can find clients who will invest in younger artists and push their career. When you have already achieved, they don't know what to do. They don't have those stages of investment, so you really have to wait till you die. Then all the vultures come in, willing to purchase residual spirit, artifacts. In all the cases of artists that I have felt were rather minor – once they died, their works were treated as major.

How was performing Interior Scroll – the Cave *in 1995 with a group of women in a cave different to the original solo performance in 1973?*

It was much easier to do in 1995! The group of women I didn't know previously gathered in this huge, local magical cave that has a river running through it. It was an incredible feeling of being in an ancient sacred space, but it was actually a mined cave where cement was developed in Rosendale, New York. Women were willing to do the action and then they were a little shy and nervous. I taught them how to do the folding and we had a whole row of different lubricants – avocado cream and apricot cream. They learned fast and it really became fun, having this sort of umbilicus. You could do the rituals: slowly pulling it out, re-folding it, and doing it again. Everybody was shy for about three minutes.

The body as a pleasurable weapon . . .

Mine is a very privileged body, because it hasn't been interfered with, but it's not a representative body for everyone. So many women have been abused, it's too dangerous to occupy this position of overt expressivity. It's a place where they actually cannot risk going themselves. My example is not useful for everyone.

Would you say that your language of representation has changed over the decades?

Would *you*?

In the main, no – only in the smallness of details.

I'd agree. I think in the smallness of details there are contemporary issues that keep shifting. I certainly have to read Lacan, Derrida, Barthes, and Foucault to know what is happening to the critical minds around my work.

Is the body your most significant contribution so far?

Centering pleasure and critical analysis on the body, and insisting on the integration of language – the neutral pronoun. I have a whole file of the insane letters I wrote during my years in London to redress the balance – the exclusionary pronoun usage. Even when they were describing a woman artist, they would conclude the essay by saying, 'and for someone in this realm of development, he has distinguished himself'. Crazy stuff! Fighting for language equity and for genital sexuality, to have them become vital, where female sexuality had belonged to pornography or medical history.

How would you say that the past and present leads into the future for you? In a sense, your current re-working of Eye Body *re-visits the past in the present.*

My sense of my own experience is not linear. It's a continuum of works as a continuity of self that's a tremendous privilege, a blessing. It has to do with when I had to re-fabricate the paint table from 1963, remembering exactly where the silver lid would have dripped and left its circle on the wood. A

tremendous happiness to be able to live in this realm of what I create. . . .

It's important to you?

It's more than important; it's how you circulate your blood and your breath, so I don't know if I'm doing anything very good or very important necessarily, but there are these images that I need to look at and make, questions or issues to resolve – I seem to be relentless in thinking about things. The notes are always piled up on my desk, I don't know where they come from. I'm a terrible typist and I can't even read them, so the question is, who cares? And if someone thinks they will care, how do you get the stuff transcribed, edited, and organized? My writing forms another layer of work. No one else can do it for me. I'm very strict about every sentence, it's got to have its own coherence and weight, and potentially to be of use.

How much do you use computer technology within your work?

I've made a visual book and eighteen computer-generated prints that I permutate – I stretch my images in the computer, re-photograph them, project them, merging pixel and Benday dot, put myself in them, so that each unit becomes a perceptual examination of form and includes performative aspects. (I know that as soon as this is published, everyone will run away to try this themselves, that's how it goes.) I've also been doing collaborative videos that are installations – multi-channel, with complex layers of editing and shooting. My most recent installation work is *Known/Unknown Plague Column*, and it's about cellular pathologies. It's very tough – a physical exploration of an aspect of disease or illness.

What inspired this particular installation?

Being told that I might have a complex fatal disease and be dead in a few months if I didn't allow a lot of self-mutilating procedures, which I refused. I explored alternative therapies and I'm cured. I put the illness right into work. I got slides of my cells and blew them up, drew them, and looked at them, spoke to them and just began this immense research.

Can you describe this piece to me?

Plague Column Known/Unknown is a complex piece because it's based on the plague column – a sculpture that I photographed in an instant in a church in Vienna. I was in Vienna to install *Mortal Coils*, the memorial installation for artists who had died of various causes. Valie Export took me to this old Baroque church and in it was the most horrific sculpture I had ever seen – so astonishing. It was a wooden, chrome, over-life-sized androgynous weird looking angel with a lot of incubuses, or little floating phalli, or little angels carrying forks and staves, and under the feet of this golden-costumed, luminous, over-life-sized angelic figure was a horrible sculptured witch, all brown and red. Out of her nipples came serpents, she had a huge nose, Medusa-like hair, and the angelic figure is stabbing a huge staff into the stomach of this witch who is curled up on her back.

Supporting this horrific dialectical proposal, that raised the question for me four months later: 'Is illness the witch or is illness this sanitized patriarchal Madonna?' Is the witch the end of the history of some aspect of women's powers of the healing arts? Is that what is being destroyed by the phoney Madonna? And the photograph that I took became an immense talismanic guide in facing my own illnesses.

What was really important about it for me was a leakage of the unconscious mind of the sculptor or sculptors, because this ferocious scene is also poised on these immense voluptuous clouds. The whole base of this didactic sculpture is this spill of cloud-like shapes: they are silver; laminated wood, and they look like cocks, breasts, and cunts. Of course, that couldn't have been the explicit intention, but it was startling to me – the rhapsodic spill. . . .

Strong imagery.

Yes, and I haven't told anybody this before, so this is a little disturbing. I lied to everybody when I did the exhibit of this piece. I insisted it was just research, because it's too difficult to have everyone's fears, worries, and opinions coming in at the same time.

I understand that. I read about Plague Column, *which stated that the piece looked at cancerous disease, making me wonder what had motivated such a choice. I had assumed that it was linked to* Mortal Coils, *rather than to your own experiences. Thank you for sharing that with me. . . . You've seen immense change in the last thirty years – feminist research into history, archeology, anthropology, linguistics, biology – it's changed everything. How do you view that today?*

It's changed the potentiality for how gender, race, and class can be socially organized. But feminism and the need for equity is a unique quest: it's not a simplistic benefit to women. Feminist principles deepen any chance we might have to salvage our own planet, which is suffering the kinds of degradation – male greed, control, mechanistic, rationalistic thinking. The worst results of this rapacious dynamic has put us in a situation where younger students have no sense of a coherent future. They can't imagine that nature will still exist for them as it existed for their grandparents, as we have known it. So the threat to our basic ecological stability is immense. We are increasingly subject to control by invasive techno-power configurations.

The whole human organism is in such a bad relationship to its earth and Gaia principles. The male energy to try to save itself and to save its real relationship to the archetypal earth, the archetypal feminine, is met head-on by feminist proportions. It means that the realm of issues is increasingly vital, political, and radicalizing. If the work that interests me the most can reach its audience (because its audience is increasingly cut off at the pass), it's diverted by consumer fantasies, false narratives, and lack of access to communication systems. Our media is completely controlled by the same corporate monsters, and they are unfailingly seductive.

It's difficult, then, to make the art accessible?

Yes. It's a calculated suppression here by the reactionary right. As we all know, the arts have become the new communist dupe, the enemy within. In so far as art practice represents the uncontrollable imagination, the leakage and spillage of a contrary cultural analysis, then it relates immediately to the feminine – the feminine and the unconscious as that part of the self which will break the structures of male power and domination.

The severity of those belief systems and convictions is not fragile. We've changed everything, but we don't know what kind of destructive forces are potentially within our need to redress them. We are still living in the cream in the US and England, because we are not invaded, we are not at war. Our house will be there when we go back, and yet Yugoslavia (which was where I used to go when I lived in England to feel that I was sane, to get some down-to-earthness), has been torn apart, savaged, and there was no correct negotiable diplomatic interference.

Conflict resolution, all the basic social negotiations we should be able to do, are fucked – in Uganda, Panama, and Grenada. We are always on a little perch of privilege here, and that perch is so full of unconscious anxiety and helpless feelings. This links right back to the five, seven, or eight generations of witchcraft burnings in which generations of women who had knowledge, who owned property, who were expressive, were all destroyed. The husbands, sons, brothers, and fathers who watched them being burnt at the stake and tortured were themselves implicated. That's a huge unexpressed gynocide. We are all sitting on that one, and it certainly must unconsciously influence males' socialization structures. It's dangerous for men among men: militaristic savagery and the profitable machinery of warfare – these are our trajectories.

What is the thing that you look most forward to at the moment?

Getting paid for something. It's desperate, and people don't believe it. A young gallery dealer came here last week to look at work and he said, 'We sold one of your books.' I said, 'Yes, thank you very much, I got the cheque and I am living on it.' He got extremely grumpy and irritated, saying, 'Oh, always some crude joker.' The idea that I was living on the sale of that book really annoyed him to the point where I realized he hadn't a clue.

When I called you this week, you said that you were as distraught and overwhelmed as ever, and I thought, nothing has changed, then. Will it always be like that for you?

I would like to have got to the ocean. It's a longing to get to the ocean – to be in the waves – but I got to Winnipeg instead.

Maybe you can still get to the ocean. . . . Lucy Lippard once described you as an emissary from a goddess. Are you?

Yes, but which one?

Is it Aphrodite?

Yes, it's Aphrodite, and you must be one too. Do you know yours?

No.

Well, go home, and read a little Robert Graves, and see which one you turn up . . . and let me know!

Notes

1. This exhibit opened from 2 February to 10 May 1998 and Paul Schimmel was the main curator. The cultural historian and writer, Kristine Stiles, organized Schneemann's participation. It is a travelling exhibition from the Museum of Contemporary Art, Los Angeles, exhibiting Schneemann's photographic series 'Eye Body', and re-creation of her 1963 New York Studio. The exhibition visited the Osterreichisches Museum für Angewandte Kunst, Vienna, 17 June–6 September 1998; the Museau d'Art Contemporani, Barcelona, 15 October, 1998–6 January 1999; and the Museum of Contemporary Art, Tokyo, 8 February–25 April 1999.

2. N. Kaye, *Art into Theatre* (Harwood Academic Publishers, 1996), p. 27.

3. Organized by Dan Cameron, 24 November–26 January 1997.

Dagmar Inštitorisová and Daniela Bačová

Across Two Eras: Slovak Theatre from Communism to Independence

At the cusp of the 'eighties and 'nineties, theatre in what was soon to become the Slovak Republic had to come to terms not only with the disintegration of the communist system, but with the break-up of the former Czechoslovakia into its constituent nations. During the previous decade, the theatre had in many ways helped to undermine the decaying authoritarian regime, but now many of its practitioners found themselves disaffected by the disappointment of early ideals, and their livelihoods threatened by the loss of state funding, which had at least acknowledged the importance of theatre to the nation's cultural prestige. In this article, the authors trace the distinguishing strands of the work of major directors and writers of both the older and the younger generations, and attempt to define the changing role of theatre – not forgetting the influence of the puppet theatre tradition – as the Slovak nation seeks a renewed vitality through reclaiming its cultural past while re-defining its present. Daniela Bacová teaches English literature and drama at the Department of English and American Studies in the University of Constantine the Philosopher, Nitra, Slovakia, and is one of the editors of the journal *Dedicated Space*. Dagmar Institorisová works in the Institute of Literary Communication in the University of Constantine the Philosopher, and has just published her doctoral thesis on *Variety of Expression in a Theatrical Work*.

OUR original idea in planning this paper was to take into account only the decade from 1989 to 1999 – starting with the year of the political changes now remembered as the Czechoslovak Velvet Revolution of November 1989, which led to the establishment of an independent Slovak Republic in 1993. But we realized that if we restricted our view to the 'nineties, we would have to ignore the artistic links between the later and the earlier period: indeed, it can be argued that the Slovak theatre reached its artistic peak in the decade that preceded the political changes.

Distinguished figures of Slovak theatre life of the 'eighties have thus consolidated and continued their work during the early 'nineties and, although new figures of promise emerged in this era, only in the second half of the decade has the Slovak theatre begun to re-establish its previous intellectual, philosophical, and artistic power.

We shall also be discussing Slovak theatre as an important socio-cultural institution in the national culture that has reacted with sensitivity to the political and social changes in the country. We have decided for this reason to include puppet theatres in our survey, as these were the first to react to the different political situation by opening their premises to the public and becoming new regional cultural centres.

Our article looks first at the theatre as an institution in the 'eighties, and at the styles of the most distinguished theatre directors who continued their work in the 'nineties. We then concentrate on the major productions of the past decade, focusing on plays written and produced by a younger generation of Slovak theatremakers, and on the new theatre groups, genres, and forms they have developed. In a third section we look at puppet theatres, and their status in Slovak culture, and finally we attempt an analysis of the political and economic transformation of Slovak theatre in its relations with post-communist governments.

At the end of the 'eighties, Slovakia – then still a part of federal Czechoslovakia, with a population of five million – could legitimately boast of the state's generous arts funding policy. There was an extensive network of fifteen state repertory theatres – between them running seventeen drama and four opera ensembles, two ballet and two musical ensembles, and five puppet theatres.

These theatres had managed to establish festivals and begun to build limited international contacts. From 1973, the Academy of Music and Dramatic Arts (VŠMU) in Bratislava had organized a prestigious International Festival of Drama Schools, the 'Istropolitana Project', held biennially in Bratislava; and in the same year what has become the oldest Slovak festival of professional theatre, the 'May Theatre Festival', started in Nitra. In 1977 'Bábkarská Bystrica', an international puppet festival, began in Banská Bystrica, though currently it is more oriented towards the Viszegrad countries.[1]

The Legacy of the 'Eighties

Within the context of Eastern European politics, the 'eighties brought considerable changes in the cultural atmosphere, reflected in the weakening of ideological censorship. While the thrust of state funding during the period of 'political normalization' of the previous decade was towards strict control of the content and style of production, theatre artists were now managing to get around bureaucratic censorship by staging classical texts with a new theatre poetics – the style of production becoming highly metaphorical, and often containing coded political messages, both appreciated and desired by the audience. Thus, we witnessed a paradoxical situation in which an authoritarian state regime officially financed a culture that was becoming increasingly subversive towards its sponsors.

The loosening of censorship and party control over theatre production meant that theatres were able to experiment with the poetics and perspective of the theatre of the absurd – not that absurdist plays were permitted to appear in theatre repertoires,[2] but Slovak directors and producers were successful in bringing the perspective of 'absurdity' to Slovak stages. An absurdist style of production subverted the surface

meaning of the plays, and was able to highlight otherwise 'unspeakable' truths about the feelings and existential anxieties of audiences. The theatres thus created a kind of secret contract with their audiences, and became centres of political dissent.

The significant productions of this decade gradually broke with the linear, cause-and-effect style of psychological realism as the only official, politically acceptable artistic practice, and began rather to experiment with elements drawn from dance, music, film, and other visual arts. The ambiguity of the meaning of the dramatic action was intensified by ironic, even grotesque perspectives. The explicitness of 'socialist' realism was subverted by parody and by the radical reinterpretation of classical texts.

Parody and irony could penetrate all elements of production, including such 'sensitive' issues as national history and myth. The fragmentation of the dramatic action, destabilization of conventional beliefs about the national past, and satire on the myth of the pure and innocent Slovak villager appear in the play *Ej, Ďurko, Ďurko* (*Jánošík*)[3] written by the Slovak dramatist Mikuláš Kočan and directed by Roman Polák for the Theatre of the Slovak National Uprising, Martin, during 1987.

The traditional folk tale depicts Jánošík as a brave and just captain of the rebels, who robs the rich and gives to the poor, and in the end is hanged after being betrayed by an old woman. In Polák's production, however, this glorified hero never appears, and in the end Jánošík and the ideals that he represents are betrayed by all the villagers. The course of the plot is broken up by folk dances and songs that function as a parody of the Party's proclaimed admiration of the working class and glorification of the lives of peasants. The upstage area consisted of a glass shop window construction that directed the audience's attention to the almost filmic detail of dramatic action.

The image of Slovak village life was portrayed with a gentler, subtler irony in another interesting production of the period, a dramatization of four stories by the Slovak writer Vincent Šikula, called *Šikuliáda*, and

Scene from *Ej, Durko, Durko*, Mikulas Kocan's satire on the myth of the pure and innocent Slovak villager, directed by Roman Polák. Photo: Tibor Huszár.

first performed in the Andrej Bagar Theatre, Nitra, in 1982. The director, Jozef Bednárik, distanced the stories through a choral commentary and the use of stylized folk traditions in the visual and musical arts. In one of the stories, this was achieved by the set resembling a model of a Slovak village, in which the actors seemed like giants.

Given the constraints of the Slovak theatre in the 'eighties, a significant generation of directors began to emerge. Roman Polák, Juraj Nvota, Blaho Uhlár, Jozef Bednárik, Ľubomír Vajdička, Štefan Korenči, Matúš Oľha, Jozef Pražmári – all succeeded in developing their own personal styles, and drawing audiences to productions with a strong ethical and aesthetic message. They have concentrated on meticulous work with the space, the actor's means of expression, music, and the visual arts. We shall discuss briefly the most significant of the group.

Leading Directors of the 'Eighties

Ľubomír Vajdička appears to be the most consistent follower of Stanislavsky's realism. His style derives from a precise, rational analysis of the dramatic script and an insistence on the construction of psychologically realistic and convincing characters. Though his productions seem to have a subdued pace, their dynamism and tension are created through the actors' action and expression.

Vajdička also incorporates the functional meaning of the setting into his productions, privileging semantic stability. In Chekhov's *Višňový sad* (*Cherry Orchard*), he thus utilized the foyer of the theatre as part of the stage action. Vajdička emphasized the elements of temporality and change by having the characters bring their luggage from the space of the foyer on to the stage, only to leave it standing there until the end of the play when they took it back to the foyer. In Strindberg's *Slečna Júlia* (*Miss Julie*, Drama Ensemble of the Slovak National Theatre, Bratislava, 1986) or in Martin Sherman's *Keď tancovala* (*When She Danced*, Bratislava, 1996) he encouraged maximally realistic acting performances. He was a leading contributor to the development and modernization of Slovak puppet theatre which will be discussed later.

In contrast to Vajdička, the work of Jozef Bednárik exemplifies a significant shift from Slovak stage realism towards stronger visualization and high production values. The Slovak theatre critic Čavojský characterizes Bednárik as a director who:

has reintroduced . . . playfulness onto the stage, along with baroque decorativeness and the richness of the stage image, the diversity of genre mixing, a sharp contrast of styles, brightness, and emphasis on the visual form of the production.[4]

Bednárik's creativity and imaginative scenographic exploration of dramatic texts have become hallmarks of his late musicals and opera in the 'nineties, but were already clear in earlier productions – Andrejev's symbolist play *Život človeka* (*The Life of Man*; Theatre of the Slovak National Uprising, Martin, 1986); Lorca's *Dom Bernardy Alby* (*The House of Bernarda Alba*, Andrej Bagar Theatre, Nitra, 1979). Bednárik has become commercially the most successful Slovak director of the past decade – in particular with a series of musicals, whose economic success has not undermined either artistic quality or their underlying humanistic message.

Bednárik openly acknowledges that his roots in the folk theatre have enabled him to set definite borders between good and evil. The musicals *Fidlikant na streche* (*Fiddler on the Roof*) by Stein, Bock, and Harnick (Andrej Bagar Theatre, Nitra, 1998) and *Drakula*, by the Czech authors Svoboda, Borovec, and Hess (Note Bene Musical, Prague, 1995, and

Bratislava, 1998) were both distinguished by a precise integration of verbal, visual, and musical elements.

Roman Polák's 'Human Archetypes'

Roman Polák, considered to be among the most original of Slovak directors, produces work that is strongly rooted in the modern European theatre tradition, and shows a strong political awareness. His productions of the late 'eighties – notably of Brecht's *Baal* (1989) and Marivaux's *Dotyky a spojenia*[5] (*The Dispute*, 1989; both for the Theatre of the Slovak National Uprising, Martin) – have become recognized as among the most significant theatrical events of the decade. At this time Polák was experimenting with savagely expressionistic theatre language and a tense, extremely focused rhythm of performance.

Baal in Polák's production is an underground rock singer and a poet who is working as a boilerman.[6] He gradually climbs up the social ladder into high society, but his nihilism and alcohol addiction are inevitably self-destructive and predetermine his tragic end. The strong, expressive music by Slovak pop singer and composer Richard Müller, together with a dark and hell-like set design

Opposite Page: L'ubomír Vajdicka's production of *When She Danced*, 1996 (photo: Jana Nemcokova). This page, top: Roman Polák's production of Brecht's *Baal*, 1989 (photo: Tibor Huszár); and bottom: Jozef Bednárik's revival of *Fiddler on the Roof*, 1998 (photo: Anton Sládek).

and the dynamism of the actors' movements created a powerful theatrical experience.

Though *Dotyky a spojenia* shared with *Baal* the depiction of a world of animal sensuality, and a similar expressionistic style of acting, this was a subtler, more lyrical, and gently humorous production, in which Polák transformed an eighteenth-century sentimental comedy into a Beckettian tragi-comedy. The

action is focused on two couples, manipulated by a pair of black servants who maintain the will of their dead master. The stage is divided by a wire fence and a door through which the characters are allowed to emerge from their isolated homes. The front stage provides a space for meetings between the young couples that are full of happiness, sensuality, inner purity, and fragility; but the upstage space behind the fence represents imprisonment, manipulation, and spiritual death. In the final tableau of the play the couples are imprisoned behind the fence, and remain staring at the audience, perplexed and helpless – a tableau which carried a strong political message in the last years of the communist regime.

In her study of Polák, Jana Bžochová-Šmatláková points out the 'attacking' quality of the style through which he creates characters, stripped of all social conventions, as 'human archetypes', representatives of a certain perspective. She characterizes Polák's style as rough and expressionistic, with its stress on irony, hyperbole, a fast pace, and a mixture of heterogeneous elements in his preferred genres of farce and grotesque.[7]

The typical features and themes of the work of Juraj Nvota are a soft and gentle humour, an understanding of human weaknesses, an intense spirituality, and a focus on social outcasts (whether idealists or swindlers) who are seeking personal fulfilment in a hostile social world. The most outstanding of his recent productions – *Armagedon na Grbe* (*Armageddon at Grb*, 1993) and *Macocha*

(*Stepmother*, 1996; both staged by Divadlo Astorka-Korzo '90, Bratislava) – were both the work of contemporary Slovak dramatist Rudolf Sloboda; and in both, as Podmaková points out, the audience is 'carried on the waves of reality, dreams, sensations, oscillating between the grotesque, cruelty, and the tragic'.[8] Nvota deals with the issues of apocalypse and the prospects for life in a new earthly paradise.

The central character of *Armageddon at Grb* is Woman – an ambiguous figure, a victim of evil and an alcohol addict, whose son commits suicide, and who is abused by her husband and suffers a gang-rape. *Stepmother* also focuses on its female characters – three young women who are slightly mentally challenged but whose desire for love and being loved is gently touching and painful. Both plays effectively combined philosophical and lyrical levels of meaning for their audiences.

The Work of Blaho Uhlár

Blaho Uhlár, one of the most controversial Slovak directors of the 'eighties, went on to become a leading personality in Slovak alter-

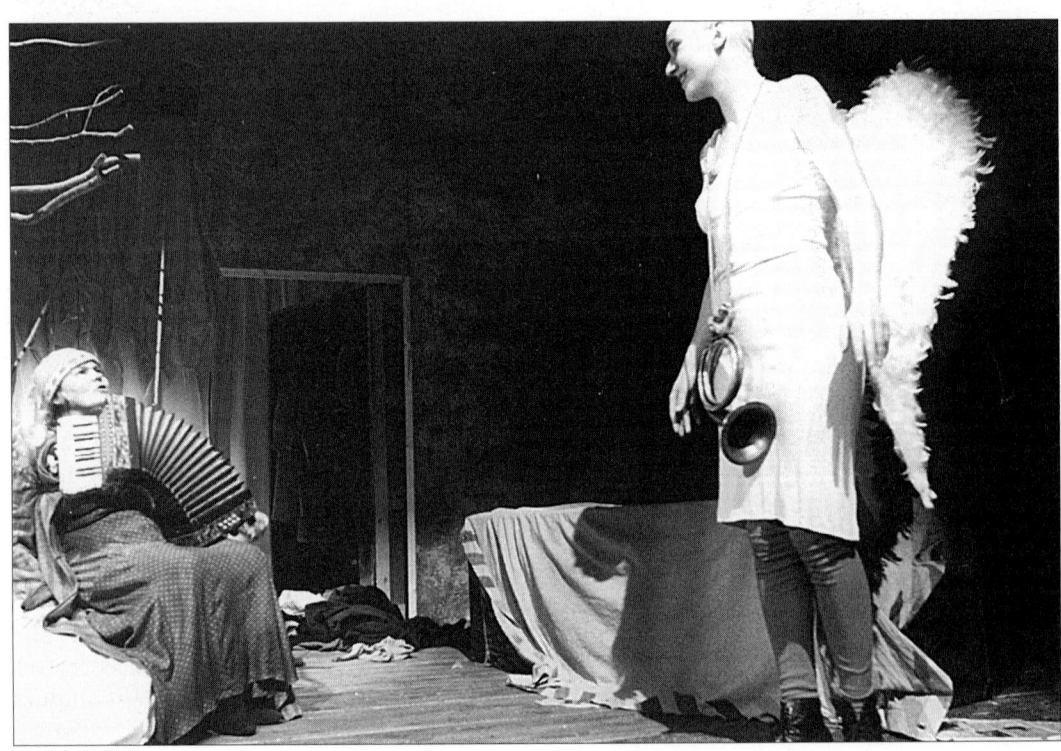

Opposite Page: Rudolf Sloboda's *Armageddon at Grb*, directed by Juraj Nvota, 1993 (photo: Matús Olha). Above: Roman Polák's revival of Marivaux' *La Dispute*, 1988 (photo: Tibor Huszár).

native theatre before, in 1991, setting up the first non-state funded theatre – STOKA, which means 'sewer'. The characteristics of his poetics – often the result of collaboration – can be traced already in the productions of the late 'eighties – notably *Predposledná večera* (*The Last But One Supper*, 1989) and *Téma Majakovský* (*The Subject is Mayakovsky*, 1987; both for the Theatre for Children and Youth, Trnava).

Both of these works were fragmentary narratives with rich visual elements, created in collaboration with the painter Miloš Karásek. The actors wore masks, ranging from the abstract to the symbolic-anthropomorphic. *The Last But One Supper*, alluding to the biblical betrayal, created a Kafkaesque atmosphere of existential absurdity in which the characters are waiting for a decision to be made by 'someone behind the door' who will become Judas, the traitor. *Téma Majakovský* comprised fragments of Mayakovsky's poems interwoven with biographical events.

Uhlár's productions of the 'nineties – *Impasse* (1991), *Dyp inaf* (*Deep Enough*, 1991), *Slepá baba* (*Blind Man*, 1992), and *Tváre* (*Faces*, 1997) – are examples of his nonconformist theatre approach which is largely non-verbal, with structures fragmented and linked by the association of images. McConnell calls Stoka's productions 'existential postmodernism', citing their concern with the 'spheres of very soft, delicate, subtle relationships and moments of human existence',[9] and in an interview for the Slovak theatrical journal *Divadlo v medzičase* Uhlár emphasizes his desire to create in his work 'authentic experience' through which the audience can 'modify and re-evaluate' their beliefs and values.[10]

Theatrical life during the last period of the communist regime was also significantly influenced by the non-professional theatre which, though still having state funding, suffered less strict censorship. The situation was utilized by such a figure as Jozef Bednárik, who in the 'eighties worked closely with an amateur theatre group Z-divadlo from Zeleneč (a west Slovak village near Trnava), whose performances aroused the interest of professional theatremakers with themes, scenography, and visual and textual reinterpretation of adapted texts. Examples, both from 1981, were their adaptations of two novelettes – Guy de Maupassant's *Boule de suif* as *Guľôčka*,[11] and Kafka's *Premena* (*Metamorphosis*) as *Otem jako sa ráz zobudzil pán Gregor Samsa ve svojej postely a ziscil, že sa premenil na obludný hmyz* (*The Story of Mr Gregor Samsa's Wakin' Up and Findin' Out He Is a Monster Insect*).

Theatrical Figures since 1989

The past decade has been full of paradoxes, partial achievements, and intermittent backlashes. Slovak theatremakers have enthusiastically worked with scripts that for various reasons could not be staged in the communist era. After twenty years the work of Václav Havel has appeared on Slovak stages, together with the plays of Slovak dramatists such as Leopold Lahola (after thirty years), Peter Karvaš, Ladislav Mňačko – notably with *Čistka* (*Purge*) – and others. At the start of the 'nineties Slovak audiences could see revivals of plays of absurdist playwrights and western European dramas by, among others, Boris Vian, Tom Stoppard, Alfred Jarry, Guillaume Apollinaire, Paul Claudel, and Michel de Ghelderode.

Soon afterwards, Slovak plays influenced by such European dramas emerged. Štefan Korenči, in collaboration with Róbert Mankovecký, created a production based on Beckett's *Waiting for Godot* under the title *Čakanie na Bohoša* (*Waiting for Bohosh*, Theatre of the Slovak National Uprising, 1992), in which two couples remain lonely Beckettian clowns, whose love, suffering, and despair can never be relieved, yet whose relationships are darkly, mystically interconnected. The set is designed as a road with two ends (the entrance and exit being concealed by a mirror), through which a messenger comes and leaves. But while in Beckett the messenger is a boy, in Korenči's production it is an unattractive woman made up like Marilyn Monroe, who announces Bohosh's failures to arrive with a dancing walk and cynical tone.

Others among the generation of theatremakers to emerge in the 'nineties include Jozef Gombár, Silvo Lavrík, Rastislav Ballek, Marián Pecko, and Michal Hatina, who continue to build on the achievements of the Slovak theatre of the past while seeking their own style. This generation expresses a strong belief in theatre, and their work shows great potential for the future. Moreover, during the second half of the decade, the more established theatre directors such as Nvota, Vajdička, and Polák, have started to emerge from their disillusion with early cultural developments after the revolution, and to create shows artistically and intellectually almost equal to their work at the end of the previous decade.

Blaho Uhlár's production of *Faces*, 1997 (photo: Ctibor Bachraty).

Adaptation and Collaboration

New productions continue to be characterized by fragmentation of plots into units, presenting a problem from a number of perspectives, while an increasing number of plays are being collaboratively written. As an example of both trends we might mention *Vajanský: Pustokvet* (*Vajansky: a Lonesome Flower*, Theatre of the Slovak National Uprising, Martin, 1997), whose episodic script was written by Rastislav Ballek (also a director of the production) and Martin Kubran, from the works of an important Slovak novelist and essayist of the nineteenth century, Svätozár Hurban Vajanský. The play was staged at a slow pace through distortions of time, numerous flashbacks, and simultaneously performed events. It may be numbered among those in which the young Slovak cultural community is seeking self-identity[12] and re-defining its own cultural heritage.

Another example of heterogeneous narrativity of dramatic plot was the rock cabaret created by young Slovak playwright Martin Čičvák, *Dom, kde sa to robí dobre* (*The House Where They Do It Well*, Drama Ensemble of the East Slovakian State Theatre, Prešov,

1996), directed by Michal Hatina. Dealing with the themes of drug addiction, prostitution, friendship, and manipulation, the cabaret was aimed at the younger generation of theatregoers, and Lehuta defined its form as 'an expressive montage and collage of signs, parts, and fragments, and their surprising meanings'.[13]

The collaboration between Roman Polák and the inventive and intellectually challenging new playwright Karol Horák has resulted in the production of postmodern intertextual works that express radical social satire. In *Divný Janko – Apokalypsa podľa Janka Kráľa* (*Strange Janko – Apocalypse According to Janko Kráľ*, Theatre of the Slovak National Uprising, Martin, 1994), Horák portrays a historical figure, Janko Kráľ' (1822–76), a poet and romantic revolutionary, but without romantic pathos. In *Nebo, peklo, Kocúrkovo* (*Heaven, Hell, Kocúrkovo*, Slovak National Theatre, Bratislava, 1995) he adapted the work of another nineteenth-century writer, the post-romantic playwright and novelist Jonáš Záborský, while remaining faithful to the satirical and realistic traditions of the nineteenth-century drama. In his essay on Horák's plays, Palkovič remarks on 'a postmodern plurality in the time and spatial stratification of the peripeteia and a varied mixture of elements coming from medieval comic culture, baroque decoration . . . [and] folk theatre, including carnivalization of the whole'.[14]

Two contemporary productions by young theatremakers received particular though not always complimentary notice. Laco Kerata's *Večera nad mestom* (*Dinner Above the City*, Andrej Bagar Theatre, Nitra, 1997), directed by the Czech director Jan Antonín Pitínský, attempted to translate the musical form of the sonata for theatre performance. The play itself, which experiments with a highly stylized approach to the actors' movement and voices, consists of three independent units that portray three different couples in three different time and spatial dimensions.

While *Večera nad mestom* has been successful with its audiences, a revival of Nestroy's *Povraz s jedným koncom* (*A Rope with One End*, Andrej Bagar Theatre, Nitra, 1996), directed by Soňa Ferancová (the only woman director of note so far to have emerged in the Slovak theatre) has received mixed reactions from critics and audiences alike – some criticizing the director for being superficial and an 'aesthete' unconcerned with deeper meaning, others praising her for taking a risk and attempting to change prevailing views on theatre and performance.[15]

From the point of view of dramatic form and expression, the plays of the 'nineties show a strong desire to break away from closed, cause-to-effect unity of action to an open, fragmentary narrative that aspires to simultaneous utterance. In this sense, the theatre continues to develop ways of staging that first arose in the 'eighties: but in its turning to aestheticism there is also evident a reaction to the communist ideology that was forcing artists to accept a single perspective and style. Contemporary Slovak plays have become highly lyrical and philosophical, some beginning almost to resemble poems in performance.

New work is often based on texts from the national past (usually on a variety of them), drawn especially from the romantic and post-romantic periods of the nineteenth century which were especially significant for the development of the Slovak self-identity and national culture. A postmodern intertextual perspective and a radical re-writing of the national and foreign classical texts with the aim of re-interpreting them have become distinguishing features in the late 'nineties.

The last decade has also seen the revival of genres and theatre forms that were not allowed under communist censorship. These include pantomime, cabaret, dance theatre, popular theatre, open-air theatre, and street performance. Moreover, new theatres have been established, with a variety of state or private or community-funded support. In Nitra, Ondrej Spišák set up a street theatre, Teatro Tatro, that from 1990 began to revive older traditions; a notable production, *Minas Thirit: Minas Morgul*, was based on episodes from Tolkien's novel, *Lord of the Rings*.

In Bratislava, Milan Sládek established an International Institute of Movement Theatre, Divadlo Aréna, that has since 1996 regularly hosted the only European festival of mime, *Kaukliar*. Two new theatres were established in Bratislava in 1990 – the Divadlo Astorka-Korzo '90 and Štúdio S, which have since become the leading stable ensembles. Two notable directors, Juraj Nvota and Roman Polák, have emerged from Divadlo Astorka-Korzo '90, while Štúdio S is the base for two highly intellectual actors – the 'philosopher-clowns' Milan Lasica and Július Satinský, neither of whom could publicly perform under the communist regime because of their strong anti-totalitarian views.

Bratislava, the one large city in Slovakia, also has two 'writers' theatres': Divadlo a.ha, established by Štefan Korenči, and GUnaGU, led by Viliam Klimáček, both of which have drawn some fine actors from state theatres. In 1992 a Romany theatre, *Romathan*, was also established in the East Slovak city of Košice, which has a strong Romany population.

The Puppet Theatre in the 'Nineties

The past decade has seen the puppet theatres widen their range and direct their work towards the teenage population. As well as introducing new themes, many have begun to experiment with different forms of staging and usage of space. In contrast to the mainstream theatre of the early 'nineties, puppet theatre productions have become more innovatory, collaborative, and risk-taking – their vision directed to the future while the big establishment theatres have been looking back to the past. Though the primary interest of the puppet theatres continues (as in the preceding era) to lie in productions for children, they are seeking new forms to deepen the connection between puppetry and 'legit' theatre components. Many have also become regional centres of youth culture, opening their premises to various club activities.

The most highly praised production of recent years has been the 1995 version of *Faust* (Puppet Theatre, Nitra) based on the texts of Marlowe's *Doctor Faustus* and of Goethe's *Faust*, as adapted for the theatre by Ondrej Spišák (also a director of the play) and Ivan Gontko. Their contemporary Faust is an easygoing and irresponsible young man whose impatient and momentary desire for knowledge is sustained by Mephistopheles as he leads Faust to an illusory world of drug addiction, and later to suffering and death. The power of the performance is underlined by a live rock band that emerges from the pit and announces one minute's silence for all the Fausts who have died as drug victims.[16]

One of the most stable and progressive puppet theatres, the Puppet Theatre at the Crossroads, is based in Banská Bystrica in the central part of Slovakia. Under the guidance of Iveta Škripková, this has developed an interesting repertoire, and productions which are praised for their unconventional style. The theatre is one of the very few in Slovakia that has changed a conventional proscenium stage into a multifunctional area and has started to concentrate on creative work with children. It is also one of the first theatres to have access for disabled people and to produce performances targeted at the handicapped audience. The company also works with deaf and dumb actors.

The Outlook for Slovak Theatre

Despite great expectations and some vital theatrical achievements in the 'nineties, the decade has not seen the creation of a cultural climate favourable or supportive to theatrical production. Sudden political and economic changes have led to a reduction in theatre audiences, and many experienced theatre-makers have been attracted by commercially more attractive openings in advertising or dubbing. The artistic crisis of theatremakers at the beginning of the period resulted in a loss of inner motivation and belief in the power of theatre's voice, and the situation worsened with the breaking up of the old Czechoslovakia, when the new Slovak political administration[17] began an economic transformation of culture intended to strengthen its own position and weaken the social (and therefore political) status of theatre. This started in January 1996, ostensibly in the interests of reducing the state budget, but in fact diverting finances for culture into the setting up of regional centres with politically appointed intendants. At the same time, the theatres lost the right to decide for themselves how to spend the state-assigned budget.

The post-communist political regime first directed its efforts to the destruction of the puppet theatres, because of their popularity as independent cultural centres – and also their vulnerability, since their members of staff were people without the high public profile of some state theatremakers. Tension increased in the spring of 1997, when in protest against state interference the puppet theatres went on a strike initiated by the Puppet Theatre in Nitra, with the catastrophic result that the intendant for the Nitra region forced the management and many members of the staff to leave, and in the autumn of that year ordered that the facade of the theatre be stripped of its paintwork and artwork, and 'redecorated' – as the 'before' and 'after' illustrations overleaf all too clearly show.

Another example of the antipathy of this administration to theatre was the financial plight of the Theatre of the Slovak National Uprising in Martin, which was an openly pro-federal institution.[18] By the autumn of 1998 the management had no finance for salaries or heating, telephones were blocked, and plays were performed with minimum

The facade of the Puppet Theatre in Nitra, before (top) and after the punitive 'redecoration'.

production costs. At the same time the East Slovak State Theatre that was established by merging two independent ensembles, with the idea of saving money, ended the first half of 1999 with a debt equivalent to £300,000.

After the elections in autumn 1998 the cultural policy of the state has changed, and the financial independence of theatres has been restored. Though financial and moral damage has been severe, we hope the theatres will regain the confidence to speak out and command audiences with original and powerful productions.

Notes and References

1. The Viszegrad countries are Poland, Hungary, the Czech Republic, and Slovakia. The 'nineties have also brought a new theatrical event, 'Divadelná Nitra' – an international festival usually held in September in Nitra.

2. In the 'seventies no play by any 'absurdist' writer could be performed on the Slovak stage, and a similar prohibition applied to many other modern dramatists. Dürrenmatt's *Der Besuch der alten Dame*, directed by Roman Polák, was thus performed for the first time in November 1989.

3. Juraj Jánošík is an historical figure whose legend could be compared to that of Robin Hood.

4. Ladislav Čavojský, 'Shakespeare-Mania and Shakespeare Magic', in Andrej Maťašík, ed., *Slovak Theatre*, trans. Oľga Ruppeldtová (Bratislava: National Theatre Centre, 1997), p. 38.

5. The production received the Critics' Award at the Edinburgh Festival in 1991.

6. Through the choice of this profession for Baal, the audience immediately understood the coded political message, since Czech and Slovak intellectuals and political dissidents often worked in similar professions. The set designer Jozef Ciller was a laureate of the Prague Quadrennial (Gold Medal, 1975, 1983) and Triennial in Novy Sad (Gold Medal, 1981). He and Jan Zavarsky are the most significant representatives of the *aftervychodil* generation of the 'eighties. Ladislav Vychodil received the Gold Medal in Sao Paulo in 1965.

7. Jana Bžochová-Šmatláková, 'Ataky režiséra Romana Poláka', *Slovenské Divadlo*, No. 2 (1987), p. 168–70.

8. Dagmar Podmaková, 'The Drift of Slovak Drama in the 1990s', in Andrej Maťašík, ed., *Slovak Theatre*, op. cit., p. 15.

9. Lauren McConnell, 'Postmodernist Theatre in Post-Communist Slovakia', in Tibor Žilka, ed., *Tracing Literary Postmodernism* (Nitra: University of Constantine the Philosopher, 1998), p. 192.

10. Interview in *Divadlo v medzičase*, III, No. 4 (December 1998).

11. The Z-Theatre took part in the international amateur theatre festival in Monaco in 1980 with its production of *Don Juan*. 'Guľôčka' achieved a major success at the International Festival of Amateur Theatres in Kanawaga, Japan, in 1985.

12. Anna Grusková, 'Mladí divadelníci o bíde slovenského intelektuála' ('Young Slovak Theatremakers on the Poverty of a Slovak Intellectual'), *Svět a divadlo*, No. 6 (1997), p. 57–61.

13. Emil Lehuta, 'Odvážny model Východoslovenského divadla' ('A Courageous Model of the Eastern Slovakian Theatre'), *Teatro*, II, No. 12 (1996), p. 39.

14. Pavol Palkovič, 'Portrét dramatika' ('The Portrayal of a Dramatist'), in *Teatro*, IV, No. 9 (1998), p. 27.

15. For example, Božena Čahojová believes that this performance might hasten desirable changes in the production and acting style of the drama company of the Andrej Bagar Theatre in Nitra, as well as bringing new postmodern perspectives into the productions of the state-funded main theatres. See Eva Čahojová, *Odvážnym čas žičí* ('Time Is Generous to the Brave Ones'), *Teatro*, II, No. 6 (1996), p. 4–5.

16. Ida Polívková-Hledíková, 'Lekcia Faust od Bábkového divadla v Nitre' ('Faust with a Moral by Puppet Theatre in Nitra'), *Národná obroda*, 23 March 1995, p. 6.

17. This was especially true of the government led by Vladimír Mečiar from 1994 to 1998.

18. The term pro-federal means not only disagreement with the split but also refusal to take part in the hate-inducing political campaign against Czechs.

Brian Roberts

Whatever Happened to Gay Theatre?

With hopes for a repeal of Clause 28 poised for imminent realization or disappointment, a successful European challenge to Britain's policy on gays and lesbians in the armed forces, and an overwhelming House of Commons vote to equalize the gay 'age of consent', gay issues are high in the public consciousness. But to what extent are these political events being reflected in contemporary theatre? In this article, Brian Roberts considers the fluctuations in gay visibility, and asks what happened to the gay theatre that sprang to prominence in the 'eighties. He situates the best of present gay theatre work as standing in a critically defining role to mainstream theatre culture, not only through its political conscientizing of 'queer' and theatricality, but also in its opposition to an assimilationist gay subculture. Brian Roberts lectures in Drama and Theatre at Goldsmiths College, University of London, and is presently revising his book *Artistic Bents: Gay Sensibility and Theatre* for publication.

RECENTLY, a colleague asked me 'Whatever happened to Gay Sweatshop?' as if the company and, by implication, a gay presence in the theatre had suddenly disappeared. Yet it was only five years ago that Milton Shulman's column in the *Evening Standard* (30 September 1994) was headlined, 'Stop the Plague of Pink Plays', while *The Independent* had an article entitled 'Off the Straight and Narrow' about the 'extraordinary proliferation of plays about gay men on the London stage'.[1] By 2 October, *The Sunday Times* was reporting 'Critics Clash as Gay Plays invade the West End'.

The language of the reportage is interesting in itself, from Shulman's homophobic use of 'plague', redolent of the blame psychology of the early AIDS crisis, to the *Sunday Times*'s use of 'invade', clearly a subtextual reference to an apparently forceful 'promotion of homosexuality' which was the keynote to the infamous Clause 28 of 1988.[2] Ironically, in the same year as Shulman's attack, a revised edition of John Crum's book *Acting Gay* dismissed gay theatre in Britain in the following paragraph:

I devote the great majority of this chapter to American gay drama because British drama, gay and straight, seems to be in a worse slump than the British economy. The parlous state of gay drama only reminds us that, despite the efforts of radical theatre groups in the 'seventies and 'eighties, a tradition of affirming gay drama never developed in Great Britain. The gay presence on the British stage is greatly the result of American imports.[3]

For Crum, the primary duty of gay drama seems to be to present positive ('affirming') gay images. In acknowledging the radical theatre of the 'seventies and 'eighties, a clear reference to Gay Sweatshop, he appears to ignore the funding problems experienced by that company during the period, and more significantly does not seem aware of the evolving face of gay subculture in the decade that followed.

This 'peek-a-boo' phenomenon in relation to gay subculture is not new, dependent as it is on the vagaries of fashion, the commercial and exploitative possibilities of the so-called 'pink pound', and the degree to which the liminality of gay subculture impinges on or is allowed to encroach into the territory of the mainstream. When, for example, did you last see any promotional material for safer sex practice outside of the gay press, and just how pervasive has the homoeroticized, sculpted male body become as an advertising motif? What this pattern of disappearance/reappearance does perhaps indicate is the changing relationship both between a gay subculture and the dominant culture and within the gay subculture itself.

Andrew Sullivan, in his analysis of pre-AIDS western society, saw a complicit pact between the dominant culture and gay subculture, where 'homosexuals could do what they wanted so long as they didn't invade the heterosexual sphere'.[4] His book, *Virtually Normal*, argues a politics of assimilation supported by civil rights and equality legislation and against the false security of the gay ghetto. Some of his argument for this can be seen in a history of gay theatre in Britain, where much of the work produced in this period was either developed by Gay Sweatshop or played only in small gay-friendly spaces – the Drill Hall, the Bush, the Latchmere, the Finborough Arms, the King's Head.

Where individual plays succeeded in breaking into the mainstream, they were supported by a larger name: Ian McKellen in *Bent* (1979), Tony Sher in *Torch-Song Trilogy* (1985), Martin Sheen in *The Normal Heart* (1986). Ironically, those three examples (with the honorable exception of Martin Sherman and *Bent*) bear out Crum's assertion about 'American imports'. Crum probably could not have predicted the outcry of 1994 against a seemingly sudden swell of gay drama, but the responses of some of those critics certainly reinforce Sullivan's analysis of a tacit pact, now broken through an 'invasion' of gay-themed drama onto the mainstream stages of the dominant culture's West End.

The Response to 'Clause 28'

The initial rallying-point for that upsurge in gay visibility in Britain was the ill-judged legislation which has become known as Clause 28. Ian McKellen came out as 'one of them', protests were organized in many theatres, and Philip Hedley announced a production of Lorca's surrealist and poetic play of forbidden love, *El Publico*, at the Theatre Royal, Stratford East, as a direct challenge to the powers of the Local Government Act and the notion of 'intentionally promoting homosexuality'.

By chance, Philip Osment's play *This Island's Mine*, produced by Gay Sweatshop, opened in February 1988. Although the play

was not written as a challenge to Clause 28, its thematic material of conflicting loyalties in a range of domestic situations was seen as an elegant, intelligent, and measured response. As Osment himself comments:

There is no doubt that Section 28[5] gave the play an added significance which meant that critics who had never before come to see the company reviewed the production.[6]

The play, written in a deceptively simple style of spoken dialogue and narrative, is very strongly actor-centred, under the influence of the work of Mike Alfreds and Shared Experience. The overlapping lives and households of the characters create a rich and complex snapshot of Britain in the late 'eighties, not least in the variety of family units and the interconnectedness of personal and political histories.

Osment's earliest idea was for a play about refugees, and there is a sense that the spectrum of characters is each in his or her own way dispossessed, through time, gender, sexuality, ethnicity, unrequited passion, place, or class; yet each, like Caliban, still feels 'this island's [also] mine'. *The Tempest*, in rehearsal and production, becomes both an ironic intertextual reference and also the holding form which brings together the coincidental linking of so many of the characters and households. There is an echo of those earliest ideas in the character of Miss Rosenblum:

Mindful of the time,
When driven out of house and homeland,
She fled the terror that swept away half
 her family.
'Last time, Mr Martin,
We were the pestilence,
Now you people are spreading a plague.
I see it.
You must watch.
You must be prepared.' . . .
'Do not think it cannot happen here.'[7]

That warning note resonated in terms both of the censorship which Clause 28 threatened and the now widespread and fuller awareness of the impact of AIDS. These two factors at the beginning of the 'nineties determined the work of gay writers, consciously or not, and fuelled an anger whose expression took many forms. Crucially, those combined threats (neither of which has gone away) also led to an increased sense of gay visibility and to a lesser extent of community and solidarity.

Culture, Subculture, and Absorption

From the early 'eighties AIDS had been ineluctably equated with homosexuality, and the visualization of gay men began to take on the proportions of a demonic and doomed menace – for example, with the British government's heavy-handed 'Don't Die of Ignorance' campaign.[8] The red ribbon, the ubiquitous western symbol of AIDS awareness, had its first public showing at a Tony Award ceremony in 1991, and rapidly became a compulsory celebrity accessory. For a brief period in the 'nineties, AIDS was even in danger of becoming *the* fashionable charity, led by Diana, Princess of Wales, and hotly pursued by Hollywood.

This high profile was occasioned and sustained by well-publicized deaths from AIDS-related illnesses of a large number of gay men working in the entertainment industry. AIDS touched the famous in a way that seemed disproportionate to the population at large, and more publicly. Awareness about the virus reached an all-time high as figures of those infected rose in what seemed to be an exponential way with the realization of the largely heterosexual pandemic in Africa. Ironically, as general awareness of AIDS increased, the reality of its effects on gay men seemed to decrease, in both the public and government consciousness, to the point where the subsidy provided to many AIDS charities has now been cut, in the misguided belief that the crisis is over.

The situation in relation to AIDS is yet another example of the 'now you see us, now you don't' syndrome, where increased visibility leads to a paradoxical disappearance, which has been described as a 'de-gaying' process. As Leo Bersani put it, 'Never before in the history of minority groups struggling for recognition and equal treatment has there been an analogous attempt, on the part

of any such group, to make itself unidentifiable even as it demands to be recognized.'[9]

The two channels through which this process of becoming 'unidentifiable' happens are assimilation into the mainstream culture and through a rapidly growing and separate or ghetto gay subculture. Neither is mutually exclusive, as it is possible for a gay man to be absorbed into the cultural mainstream (to be 'virtually normal' in Sullivan's phrase) and still enjoy the exclusively gay culture of the ghetto. Indeed, as those two ideas are frequently merged in the popular culture of music, fashion, TV, and film, any residual sense of dislocation between assimilation and the ghetto can seem to fade in a growing appearance of acceptance and tolerance. What might have been visible 'gayness' thus becomes diluted in the fashionable absorption and disappears. What matter that we have four out(ed) gay cabinet ministers, with Clause 28 still on the statute books and an unequal age of consent, if we also have *Gaytime TV*, Lily Savage hosting *Blankety Blank*, and *Sir* Elton John?

The annual Gay Pride march and rally provides something of an exemplar of this process at work. Originally formulated as Gay Pride, it became the Lesbian and Gay Pride March as a greater awareness of specific lesbian issues was acknowledged. A few years ago it became simply 'Pride' and this year it has become 'Mardi Gras'. Over the years the march and festival have grown in numbers and cost, and, in a bid to attract sponsorship and swell numbers even further the organizers have tried to shift public consciousness away from gay politics towards a more generalized sense of carnival theatre and summertime celebration.

The changing relationships within the subculture itself can best be summed up in the phrase 'postgay', as cited in Alan Sinfield's book *Gay and After*.[10] It is a sign of maturity within a comparatively young 'movement' that there are writers and playwrights who are moving beyond the defensive and 'affirming' position of gay cultural production towards a more critical, questioning stance. Several writers (Sullivan, Sinfield, Bersani) have noted that the politics of the original Gay Liberation Movement have largely shifted from the liberationist to the *ersatz* freedom of assimilation and the ghetto.

Daniel Harris, in *The Rise and Fall of Gay Culture*, sees the changes in gay culture as part of 'the accelerating pace of our assimilation into mainstream society' – towards a 'melting pot' culture in which everything becomes a 'sludgelike stew'.[11] *Anti-Gay* goes further in its attack on gay culture and the anti-critical mentality of the gay response to queer politics which, 'rather than challenge the thinking behind taxonomies of "deviant" and "normal" . . . has been to try and prove its "normality".'[12]

Between Queer and Gay

The distinction between 'queer' and 'gay' might seem redundant to those who see the terms as synonymous, but there is an important post-structural understanding which differentiates the terms and is pertinent to the study of contemporary gay subcultural production. The self-designated term 'gay' was deliberately adopted within the post-Stonewall Liberation Movement (Gay Liberation Front) as a way of acknowledging publicly a previously codified signifier used between homosexuals in a covert subculture. The defiantly appropriated term 'queer' has come to be identified with a post-AIDS consciousness and, at one level of meaning, is associated with radical, direct-action groups such as Act-Up.[13] 'Queer' deliberately rejects a perception of 'gay' as white, middle-class, affluent, and assimilated, either passing within the dominant culture or reliant on the ghetto of gay subculture. There are those who would observe that 'queer' has also echoed the gay movement in its rapid transformation from a subversive force into radical chic and a fashion statement – a seemingly willing collusion with the colonizing forces of fashionable commerce and media.

The other significant area of reappropriation of 'queer' is in the rapid expansion of Queer Studies, which developed out of the pioneering Gay and Lesbian Studies, mostly led by American academics. Queer Studies would subsume queer politics, queer cultural theory, and queer aesthetics, and argues that elements of homophobia and heterosexism may be discerned in the conflicts and contradictions which exist when 'deviant' sexuality encounters most social and cultural structures.

For both academics and activists, 'queer' gets a critical edge by defining itself against the normal rather than the heterosexual . . . [and] also allows it to draw on dissatisfaction with the regime of the normal in general. . . . We might even say that queer politics opposes society itself.[14]

The themes of sexuality and sexual energy are potent forces in so much of our cultural readings and tend to assume a normative and conformative notion of identity. Thus liberation politics, as evidenced in the Gay Movement, were concerned with the individualization of (homo)sexual identity, but assumed 'the social dominance of a system of mutually exclusive roles around sexual orientation (homosexual/heterosexual) and gender (masculine/feminine)'.[15]

This assumption was predicated on the notion that sexual orientation is the only significant difference, and either precludes or assumes an inclusion of differences based on class, race, ethnicity, age, sexual preference, and geographical location. In seeking to challenge the system through individualization, liberationists unwittingly perpetuated notions of identity fractured along binary oppositional lines, and failed to take account of other multiple differences.

The thinking which underpins Queer theory is deconstructionist, and urges a shift in focus 'from the politics of personal identity to the politics of signification'[16] – 'a view of identity as difference'.[17] But difference also implies otherness; so that, rather than attempting to construct some monolithic gay identity, we should be concerned with a deconstructive analysis of identity in relation to its *multiple* significations and possible readings.

By and large, 'gay' has not become 'queer' in the theatre, although productions such as Mark Ravenhill's *Shopping and Fucking* (1996) and Neil Bartlett's *The Picture of*

Dorian Gray (1994) are proof that the theatre does not stand outside the postmodern momentum. What is more pertinent is that the queer movement itself seems to have drawn on theatre in its understanding of sexual identity as multiple, metamorphic, and performative. It is thus significant that queer and postmodern in performance terms increasingly imply 'performance art', exemplified in the one-person show or the hybridity of multi-media work, where technology itself becomes the overwhelming feature, with a privileging of form over content.

Defining the Subcultural Tensions

These developments in gay/lesbian/queer studies raise the question of whether we can talk of a gay theatre at all. Crum talks of 'gay drama', referring to:

two kinds of plays written for two kinds of audiences. One type is the post-Stonewall play, which is written primarily for gay audiences and which speaks to their shared experience. . . . The other type of gay drama is the pre-Stonewall play written for the mainstream theatre by a homosexual playwright.[18]

The latter category includes the codified drama of Williams, Coward, Rattigan, and Orton, and is arguably not 'gay' at all. Neil Bartlett has persuasively argued[19] that the whole of British theatre is so infused with a gay sensibility that to talk about gay theatre as something particular and separate is wholly redundant. The danger of such a provocative stance is that it either trivializes gay cultural achievement in the theatre or creates the climate of complacency attacked in the post-gay arguments. And both views marginalize gay drama, condemning innovative work to small-scale, poorly financed and resourced short runs in fringe venues, few of which are visited by the major theatre critics.

In preference to the perceived binary opposition between the fringe and the mainstream, I would wish to consider the tension within gay subcultural production between the ideas of assimilation and the ghetto and those of confrontation and opposition. This is not a simplistic 'gay' versus 'queer' distinction, but a qualitative distinction between a theatre which addresses itself primarily to a mainstream gay audience and one which is more challenging – and which I would consider makes up a canon of gay (in the absence of any suitable alternative word) theatre work. This work may be influenced by the liberation politics of the early Gay Movement, by the oppositional politics of queer, or by the urge to create exciting live theatre which challenges our position and which is created out of a gay sensibility – by which I mean a way of understanding the world from a politicized gay perspective.

Let me give an example of the tension I am talking about. One of the most recent of gay plays to have enjoyed a localized success is Adrian Pagan's *The Backroom*, which was produced at the Bush Theatre in July 1999. The play, advertised as a comedy, is set in a seedy Earls Court male brothel and reflected all the fetishistic obsessions which are popularly believed to constitute gay culture – music, female icons, clubs, fashion, drugs. Much of the writing was fast and comic, operating on the level of a sexual farce, with a proportion of witty one-liners and camp exchanges.

Much the same sort of description might be applied to the critically acclaimed *My Night with Reg* (Royal Court, 1994), although the writing in Elyot's play was much better. There is a tentative romance between two of the rent boys (Charlie and Sandy) who, in an epilogue to the piece, are seen to have set up in their own escort/prostitution business. There were some insights into why this representative group of men were 'on the game', but little in the way of individual character development, which was largely confined to the stereotypical images they projected as their business personae – the 'boy next door', 'surfer boy', 'squaddie', or 'body builder'. The overriding sense was that this was a pilot for a TV sitcom, and about as dangerous as Victoria Wood's *Dinnerladies*.

Rod Dungate's *Playing by the Rules* – seen at Birmingham Rep in 1992 and the Drill Hall in 1993 – also dealt with male prostitution, but in an altogether different style, theatrically as well as thematically. The play is set in Birmingham, and its action catches up a group of young people: Danny, fifteen; Sean, seventeen; Steve, eighteen; Tony, seventeen; Ape, Tony's half-brother, nineteen or twenty; Julie, seventeen, Steve's girl-friend and Sean's best friend.

These characters survive as best they can through prostitution, petty thieving, and sharing the flat in which Sean is being kept by a local councillor. As the others explain to Danny: 'We watch out for each other. We're a family.' It is exactly that sense of re-creating a lost family which both binds them together and dictates their *modus vivendi*. In each case there is a history of familial disfunction, of rejection, of absence of love, leaving them damaged and defensive.

Steve and Danny have both been in 'The Conifers', a residential care hostel; Tony and Ape were taken into care after the suicide of their mother; Sean was thrown out by his father for being gay; and Julie is still living with an alcoholic mother. Within their surrogate family it is Steve who takes the paternal role, organizing the others and taking care of Danny, while Sean plays the maternal role, providing and supporting, aided by his friendship with Julie. It is the arrival of the fifteen-year-old Danny which provides the catalyst for the action.

In his tutelage of Danny into the life on the streets, Steve gradually realizes the falseness of his dream of a married life with Julie and, possibly seeing something of his younger self in Danny, begins to experience feelings of attraction and love for him. In doing so, he transfers his heterosexual aspirations for marriage and children into his newly discovered and painfully articulated feelings for Danny:

STEVE: I like you more than anyone I've ever met.
DANNY: More than Julie?
STEVE: Don't laugh at me.
DANNY: I'm not.
STEVE: I can't even think about no one else.[20]

Danny's eventual betrayal of Steve and the 'family' is motivated by a sense of vengeance for his wronged adolescent self and against the system of false carers. The form it takes is his involvement with King, who controls the 'rent scene'. Each of the actors, in turn, plays the role of King, emphasizing his origins and their potential future. King's connections extend beyond the Birmingham rent scene into supplying drugs and an international male prostitution business.

Danny's journey ends with him playing a youthful copy of King, recruiting boys from the same care centre from which he had absconded, turning his back on Steve's 'happy ending', and reaching out for the one thing that he has learnt: the power potential and financial rewards from the commodification of his own and others' bodies. He learns not only to play the rules of the rent scene, but to turn them into power games for his own advantage, abandoning the others to their dreams and a rapidly disintegrating 'family'.

Layers of Deprivation

Dungate suggests that the social and emotional layers of deprivation, coupled with a shrinking traditional job market and an increase in low-paid service work, begin to explain, if not justify, the 'rent scene'; but the response to the character of Danny – whose story we have followed through innocence and initiation to learning and success, with sympathy, humour, excitement, and pathos – is more complex. The final moments of the Epilogue, with this same character in a smart suit conducting his exploitative business on a mobile phone, are shocking:

> See, what I'm thinking is we're paying 'em too much. What they do for twenty, they'll do for fifteen . . . anything we ask 'em to do's a piece of piss: the kids I'm talking to are desperate for money (p. 98).

There is an evident political comment, but this is not just a 'problem-play' about male prostitution: it is a richer theatrical experience and a play about 'six people', rather than a Shavian *Mr. Warren's Profession*, in which 'the acting space is like a large mirror in which Society is reflected'. [21]

Shopping and Fucking, Mark Ravenhill's 1997 *succès de scandale*, challenges political thinking in its deliberate use of shock tactics and an action which goes beyond a monolithic focus on gay issues. This is possibly another determining factor in the distinction between assimilationist/ghetto and confrontational/oppositional gay theatre work. The former addresses itself to a gay audience and also confines itself to a gay agenda; the latter resonates both within and beyond the gay experience. Ravenhill himself acknowledges that he wants to 'disturb and provoke' with his play, but also makes the point that:

There was a slight worry . . . that it had become an event, something to be crossed off a list, that it was really more important to be there than to engage with what was being said, which was to look at what is happening to young people after seventeen years of this government.[22]

Ravenhill's cautionary note is about the dangers of his work being absorbed into the fashionable ghetto culture, rather than being more freely oppositional to the gay subculture as much as to society itself.

The key metaphor of the play, which is largely metaphor, opens and closes the production. The opening stage direction reads: 'Lulu and Robbie are trying to get Mark to eat from a carton of takeaway food.' The closing direction is: 'Mark, Robbie, and Lulu take it in turns to feed each other.'[23] This is, indeed, a play about consumption: consume or be consumed, consumer society, conspicuous consumption, the *consummatum est* of that final image. But it is also about the by-products of consumerism – waste, detritus, fall-out, junk, trash – where human intercourse becomes entirely transactional and love is an addiction: reality held at bay with 'little stories' of shopping or fucking which have replaced the metanarratives which might once have given meaning to life.

The Garden of Eden becomes a homoerotic scenario on a telephone sex line, and Chekhov's *Three Sisters* is ironically juxtaposed in a *faux* audition for a role selling drugs with the sentimental power-broker Brian. And the explicit sex scenes are made doubly shocking in the unfolding story of the abused adolescent Gary and his willing submission to his perceived destiny as victim (of the consumer system, of AIDS, of an unrequitable sexuality).

> I've got this unhappiness. This big sadness swelling like it's gonna burst./ I'm sick and I'm never going to be well. . . . I want it over. And there's only one ending.[24]

The bleakness of this vision is only partially relieved by some of the darker comedy and by the acceptance of the last moments of the play, where survival seems to be about both mutual feeding and also feeding off within a 'family unit' held together by its collective narrative. The consumption/waste nexus becomes a terrible indictment of capitalism in its Thatcherite form in general and the complicity of the gay subculture within a monetarist economy in particular.

Caught in the Culture of Commodification

In all three plays bodies, particularly male bodies, are commodified, packaged, and sold – for cash, for comfort, for a sense of belonging. In *Backroom* this is presented as unproblematic fact, where police raids and genital warts are occasional occupational hazards and where the primary concern is to make enough money to enjoy the sybaritic amnesia of the gay ghetto club culture (Madonna, Craig, Dallas), pay for a university education (Sandy), break from the strictures of middle-class values (Charlie), or support a young family (Paul).

None of these ideas is explored, beyond giving a little surface background to the characters, and it is as if they are hermetically sealed in this all-male environment with little reference beyond the squalid setting of the brothel and the hedonism of the gay scene. Even Charlie's complex relationship with his evidently wealthy family is subsumed in his initiation into being 'streetwise' and hence accepting this world, and in his personal/business relationship with Sandy, as if that provided the 'happy ending' which Dungate eschews in the same Epilogue form.

Both *Playing by the Rules* and *Shopping and Fucking*, however, identify and theatricalize the damage to young people caught in this commodification culture which goes beyond the immediacy of the gay subculture. The set of *Playing by the Rules* – with derelict cars, oil drums, and a structure resembling the desolate land beneath motorway flyovers – and *Shopping and Fucking*'s insistent neon signs, reinforce ideas of abandonment and waste in the former and the pressure of commercialism in the latter. Both are plays which demand a response beyond a cosy 'good night out' which seemed to be the primary intention of the *Backroom* farce.

The Work of Jonathan Harvey

Jonathan Harvey is a writer who also rejects the middle-class assumptions of 'gay', but whose work is not obviously confrontational and keeps a delicate balance between assimilationist sentimentality and a more oppositional understanding of the gay experience. *Beautiful Thing* (Bush Theatre, 1993) was a coming-out play praised and damned in almost equal measures for its 'feel-good factor'. It was remarkable for a number of reasons: the characters of Jamie and Ste (fifteen and sixteen respectively) were evidently 'under age' at a time of parliamentary deliberation about lowering the age of homosexual consent; the characters were placed in a Thamesmead housing estate and were not 'two public schoolboys punting through Cambridge in cricket whites';[25] and the ending – on a note of joyous celebration – affirmatory and heart-warming.

The play was criticized for its unreality, which spoke more about the painfulness of coming out as a gay rite of passage than the realities of parental and sibling homophobic brutality which were there in the absent characters of Ste's family, the oblique reference to AIDS, and the internalized sense of (wrong) self which emerges in Jamie's outburst: 'I'm a queer! A bender! A pufter! A knobshiner! Brownhatter! Shirtflaplifter!' The final scene was an unashamed piece of theatrical artifice, with a glitter-ball 'casting millions of dance-hall lights', the music of Mama Cass singing 'Dream a Little Dream with Me', and the two boys dancing together – simultaneously generating that warm 'feel-good' factor, but also projecting a powerful

wish-fulfilment, not just of 'if only . . . ', but also of 'why shouldn't it be like this?'

Harvey's next play, *Rupert Street Lonely Heart's Club* (Donmar Warehouse, 1995), had little of that 'feel-good' element in its focus on the psychosexual pathology of gay desire – in particular, the relationship of the two brothers Marti (gay) and Shaun (straight). The intensity of their love/hate relationship, Marti's sexual feelings for his brother, and the 'camp' interlude where they briefly meet, hiding true feelings behind the persiflage of Bette Davis dialogue, provides a powerful frame for what becomes a weakened melodrama in Marti's attempted suicide – a destructive gesture, expressive of inadequacy and loneliness.

The exploration of gay/straight masculinity takes this play out of a comfortable assimilationist category and into a problematic area for gay and mainstream audiences alike. The play, more obviously oppositional and challenging in its confrontation with masculinities, seemed to confuse gay audiences looking for more of an affirmatory 'feel-good' follow-up to *Beautiful Thing*.

Uneasy fraternal relationships seem to feature in much of Harvey's work. They reappear in a more resolved form in *Hushabye Mountain* (Hampstead Theatre, 1999). This is Harvey's AIDS play, and bears some comparison with and more than a passing resemblance to Kushner's momentous *Angels in America* (National Theatre, 1992–93). Both plays have central conceits of heaven, angels, and hallucinatory experiences *versus* domestic realities as the frameworks for their fantasias on gay themes in a time of AIDS. If the angels in *Hushabye Mountain* are less celestial and more homely, the quest is not as cosmic as the fantasy in *Angels*, where God has abandoned the earth until stasis returns.

In Harvey's play, the spirit of Daniel is in limbo on a cotton-wool cloud, unable to pass on ('or is it over?') until unfinished business with his mother, lover, and friends has been completed: centrally, the delusional lives he and his mother have led, his denial of her existence, her choice between homophobic husband and homosexual son, and retreat into temporary silence and madness.

Both are redemptive plays of reconciliation, forgiveness, and healing, but whereas Kushner's message is that of Auden's 'We must love one another or die', Harvey's is to do with letting go, moving on, and surviving. Kushner's is the bigger political picture, Harvey's more domestic; but both are richly veined, multi-threaded theatrical explorations of the realities of gay life in the 'nineties.

The time difference between the two plays makes a difference. The anger at untimely loss is there in both: the fear, the hurt, the struggle to understand, the resilient humour of camp are both common and uncommon emotions which link the plays. In Kushner there is survival (Prior) as well as death (Roy Cohn), whereas in Harvey's play the death of Danny problematizes the survival of Connor and his relationship with his brother Lee and his new lover Ben, here echoing Andrew Alty's *Something about Us* (Lyric Studio, 1995). But, more significantly, where Kushner dared to characterize Roy Cohn as part of the texture of American life in the 'eighties, Harvey, through the character of Ben, speaks some of the unspeakable truths about living with AIDS and the stabilization of combination therapies in the late 'nineties:

> I've spent the last three years thinking me time was up. Owt I did was a preparation for death. And now. Now some tosser's gone and moved the goalposts. I can't really take it all in. . . . They've closed three AIDS wards in London coz they couldn't fill the beds. . . . D'you know my dream? They'll have to change the Lighthouse into a job centre for all of us who thought we were going to die.[26]

The staging of both plays demands rapid, fluid changes of scene, with lighting and sound playing key roles. While the touring production of *Hushabye Mountain* could not command the resources of the RNT, the same sense of conscious theatricality pervaded both productions.

Theatre and Theatricality

It is probably a truism to observe that 'theatricality' is more than an unproblematic or uncontested way of describing 'theatre': there are tensions within that relationship.

A quick glance at a dictionary illustrates a growing understanding of the word 'theatrical' from the neutrality of 'pertaining to or connected with theatre' to the more loaded 'artificial; affected' and 'extravagantly or irrelevantly histrionic; "stagey"; "showy".' I would take that tension between theatre and theatricality further, and express it as a series of binary oppositions, such as: serious/frivolous; content/form; authenticity/parody; truth/illusion; reality/play; masculine/feminine; heterosexist/camp (queer); orthodox/paradox; catharsis/pleasure; verbal/pictorial; sincerity/artifice.

Mainstream theatre may have used the language of theatre, but has largely excluded theatricality from its vocabulary. Theatricality was the territory of the popular theatre of melodrama, music hall, cabaret, circus; the world of the cinema, pantomime, musical theatre, the pop concert. What is important is not the fixed meanings of those oppositions, but the slippage between them and the flexibility that that opens up. In an interview with Robert Lepage in 1992, Richard Eyre makes the observation about his work that 'it converts the commonplace into the magical and makes the magical real and accessible', and in the same interview Lepage states: 'I think there's an important word that has lost its sense in the theatre, and that's the word "playing".'[27]

This tension between 'high' and 'low' art in the theatre is not new. Shaw castigated Wilde's *The Importance of Being Earnest* for playing without a purpose – in other words, for being theatrical without due regard for theatre. Peter Brook's *A Midsummer Night's Dream* (1970) was possibly a pivotal moment of slippage between the 'high' art of Shakespeare and the 'low' art of circus skills and popular forms. Although I could not argue that all gay theatre work is informed by that quality of theatricality, much of the work which I have been identifying does seem to embrace all those understandings of theatricality in its rich sense of the possibilities of theatre – work which is multi-layered and is best understood through a sensory as well as intellectual apprehension, which is both an expression of gay sensibility and yet oppositional; which expresses something of the learned performativity of gay identity through camp (itself concerned with the slippage between the masculine/ feminine binary) and an awareness of play, parody, irony, and the periphery of the mainstream.

Theatricality and Gender Identity

Perhaps nowhere in contemporary theatre is this illustrated more clearly than in the work of Neil Bartlett. His *Night after Night* (Royal Court, 1993), *The Picture of Dorian Gray* (Lyric, Hammersmith, 1994), and *Sarrasine* (Traverse, Edinburgh, 1990; Lyric, Hammersmith, 1996) all consciously play with the metaphor of theatre and the understanding of sexual and/or gender identity. All three play with time, having an evident setting in the past, but with images and allusions that resonate in the present – most obviously in *Night after Night*, where Bartlett plays himself as a character in his father's story of musical theatre in the 'fifties.

The theatre in all three plays is literal as well as a metaphor of performed identity: the layering of costumes and backdrops to the bare walls in *Sarrasine*; the backstage life of *Night after Night*; the obliquely built set of *Dorian Gray*, blending with the ornate proscenium arch stage left but exposing the brickwork and concrete of the Lyric's outer shell stage right and soaring into the flies with a black-framed gallery for the musicians of the string orchestra who echo, counterpoint and comment on the action below.

That layering of image and meaning, the transitions from 'high' to 'low' art, the casting of established names with drag actors, invites a deconstruction of the notions of 'seeming' and 'being' not only in relation to gender and sexual identity, but also in terms of history, mythologies, performance, and an understanding of theatre itself. More acutely, Bartlett synthesizes ideas from the assimilationist/ghetto gay subculture with those of a more challenging confrontational/oppositional theatre, both intelligent *and* theatrical.

This consideration of work which might be considered as making up the canon of gay theatre doesn't take into account some of the many other talents working in the contemporary theatre: Kevin Elyot's *My Night with Reg* (Royal Court, 1994) and *The Day I Stood Still* (1998); Philip Osment's most recent plays, *What I Did in the Holidays* (1995) and *The Undertaking* (Gay Sweatshop, 1996); the work of Noel Grieg; Lindsey Kemp; Bette Bourne and Bloolips; DV8 Dance Theatre; Nigel Charnock; Matthew Bourne and Adventures in Motion Pictures – and all the many others who have attempted to move beyond the ghetto of the gay subculture to challenge the drift into assimilation and invisibility by articulating the concerns of a gay minority through a politicized gay sensibility and a theatricalized voice which speaks to more than just a gay audience.

To answer my own question, what happened to gay theatre is that it grew up and became more than the 'affirming gay drama' whose absence Crum noted in 1992. The best of gay theatre work in the last decade has become closer kin to the radical theatre of its origins. Despite (or because of) the censorship of Clause 28, the debilitating effects of multiple bereavement from AIDS-related deaths, homophobic attacks in the press, and a changing perception of 'gay' itself, the theatre continues to be a place where vital issues within and beyond the gay community can be expressed in a range of forms – magical and moving, shocking and humorous, sensuous and thought-provoking.

Notes and References

1. Paul Taylor, *The Independent*, 26 September 1994.

2. This section of the Local Government Act of 1988 is still referred to by its original title of 'Clause 28' and states that: 'A local authority shall not: a) Intentionally promote homosexuality or publish material with the intention of promoting homosexuality. b) Promote the teaching in any maintained school of the acceptability of homosexuality as a pretended family relationship.' The section/clause remains on the statute books, unreformed and unchanged.

3. John M. Crum, *Acting Gay: Male Homosexuality in Modern Drama* (New York: Columbia University Press, 1992; revised, 1994), p. 281.

4. Andrew Sullivan, *Virtually Normal* (London: Picador, 1995), p. 122.

5. 'Clause 28' is still the most commonly understood description of the notorious paragraphs. Strictly, when

it passed into law it became 'Section 28' of the Local Government Act, 1988.

6. Philip Osment, ed., *Gay Sweatshop: Four Plays and a Company* (London: Methuen, 1989), p. lxiv.

7. Osment, ibid., p. 88.

8. Simon Garfield's *The End of Innocence: Britain in the Time of AIDS* (London: Faber, 1994) is a compelling account of the history of the virus in Britain.

9. Leo Bersani, *Homos* (Cambridge, Mass.: Harvard University Press, 1995), p. 31–2.

10. Alan Sinfield, *Gay and After* (London: Serpent's Tail, 1998), p. 115.

11. Daniel Harris, *The Rise and Fall of Gay Culture* (New York: Ballantine Books, 1997), p. 4.

12. Toby Manning, 'Gay Culture: Who Needs It?' in Mark Simpson, ed., *Anti-Gay* (London: Cassell, 1996), p. 100.

13. Act-Up (the AIDS Coalition to Unleash Power) was formed in 1989, based on the American organization Outrage. It was/is an *ad hoc* pressure group which uses theatrical strategies to raise public awareness about Queer issues.

14. Michael Warner, ed., *Fear of a Queer Planet: Queer Politics and Social Theory* (Minneapolis: University of Minnesota Press, 1993), p xxxi–vii.

15. Steven Seidman, *Identity and Politics in a 'Postmodern' Gay Culture*, in Warner, op. cit., p. 129.

16. Ibid., p. 130.

17. Diana Fuss, *Essentially Speaking* (London: Routledge, 1989), p. 102–3.

18. Crum, op. cit., p. xvi.

19. Neil Bartlett, 'What Mainstream?', paper delivered *in absentia* at the 'Queering the Pitch' conference, Manchester, September 1994.

20. Rod Dungate, *Playing by the Rules*, in Michael Wilcox, ed., *Gay Plays: 5* (London: Methuen, 1994), p. 76.

21. Dungate, ibid., p. 99.

22. Mark Ravenhill, interviewed by Tilly McAuley, *Gay Times*, April 1997.

23. Mark Ravenhill, *Shopping and Fucking* (London: Methuen, 1997).

24. Ibid., p. 83.

25. Jonathan Harvey, in an afterword to *Beautiful Thing*, in Wilcox, ed., *Gay Plays: 5*, op. cit., p. 210.

26. Jonathan Harvey, *Hushabye Mountain* (London: Methuen, 1999), p. 94–5.

27. Robert Lepage, in discussion with Richard Eyre, quoted in Michael Huxley and Noel Witts., eds, *The Twentieth-Century Performance Reader* (London: Routledge, 1996), p. 238–41.

Joanna Ostrowska

'My Future Plan? To Die': Grotowski's Last Visit to Wrocław

After fifteen years absence, Jerzy Grotowski returned to Wroclaw on 6 March 1997, for the presentation of an award for his contribution to Polish Culture made by the Cultural Foundation's chairman, Stefan Starczewski. Grotowski was accompanied by his protégé and collaborator, Thomas Richards, and went to great lengths to establish Richards's equal and often major contribution to the laboratory work at Pontedera in Italy, which they had been jointly leading since 1986. This work has eschewed publicity, has never sought an audience, and has only been witnessed by chosen groups of sympathetic experts, who have been felt necessary at times for its validation. Initiated and sustained because of the reputation which had accrued to Grotowski during the various phases of his earlier career, the danger was that it might cease to attract support on the demise of its principal validator – which, as one of Grotowski's replies at the Wroclaw meeting anticipated, sadly occurred last year. By acknowledging the functional and artistic importance of Thomas Richards, Grotowski here establishes the argument for his work – described in detail in Richards's own *At Work with Grotowski on Physical Actions* (Routledge, 1995) – to be continued, as the status of the old master passes to the new. Joanna Ostrowska, who is currently working at the Institute of Cultural Studies, Adam Mickiewicz University, Poznan, here offers her own impressions of the Wroclaw meeting.

WHEN I participated in a seminar at New York University on Jerzy Grotowski's period of theatre work, back in February 1993, Andre Gregory was one of the speakers. He asked us not to take down any notes while he spoke. 'If you only listen to me, you'll remember what is most important for you. What is the point of trying to recall from notes what's not important to you?' So I decided to follow this advice during the meeting with Jerzy Grotowski and his collaborator Thomas Richards, which took place at the Theatre Polski in Wrocław on 3 March 1997. I didn't take notes, so this is a report of what still seemed, a few days later, 'most important for me'.

Richards was given full rights as co-host at the meeting. Grotowski made it pointedly clear several times that they were presently collaborators and not master and pupil ('Thomas Richards knows more concerning the vibratory songs than me') and he frequently passed on to Richards questions addressed to him.

'All Poland' came to this meeting with Grotowski in Wrocław. I noticed famous directors: Tadeusz Bradecki and Jerzy Jarocki; Lech Raczak, former leader of the Teatr Osmego Dnia, with a few actors from this company; Wojciech Krukowski from Akademia Ruchu; Włodzimierz Staniewski from Gardzienice; almost the whole ensemble from Kana in Szczecin; Jolanta Cynkutis. . . . And there were Professors Osiński, Kelera, Degler, a few dozen people from the circle of young alternative theatre, theatre critics, and many others, more or less well-known. 'The old theatregoers' were saying that a gathering such as this couldn't have taken place for any other theatrical occasion.

There was an atmosphere characteristic of meetings of high society. While the session participants were sluggishly taking their seats in the audience, the numerous news reporters, gathered in front of the stage, suddenly ran towards someone getting into a seat in the first row. It turned out that it was Andrzej Wajda.

He became very distinctly present once more during the evening when he asked Grotowski a question. The whole audience froze, waiting to hear what the famous film and theatre director might ask Grotowski. He asked if it was possible to move a table lamp a little bit because it was blocking his view of the meeting's hero. Grotowski did this in person. Then there was a voice from the other side whose owner complained that he had now got the lamp in his view. Unfortunatly this person didn't have Andrzej Wajda's force of authority.

The meeting began with the presentation to Grotowski of the Award of the Grand Cultural Foundation by Stefan Starczewski, the Foundation's chairman. In a short speech Starczewski naturally stressed Grotowski's contribution to Polish culture. If Grotowski is really such an ironist as he is said to be, then reality is his worthy partner, and its malicious chuckle clearly reverberated while the chairman spoke these words. Twenty-eight years had intervened between the last premiere of the Laboratory Theatre and the recognition and conferring upon Grotowski of an award in the field of direction by the magazine *Theatre*, the official organ of the Artists' Association of the Polish Stage. Then, fifteen years of Grotowski's absence from Poland were to pass before he was honoured by 'Polish Culture' which earlier, through the writing (not only) of its greater or lesser official representatives, had 'proved' the charlatanism of the creator of the Laboratory Theatre.

After receiving the award, Grotowski presented his plan for the evening's meeting: first to come was an introduction by Thomas Richards, then a film by Chiquita Gregory on *Action*, and finally, questions. 'If you would like to ask Mr Richards any questions, even if you know English I would request you to ask your questions in Polish. There is a translator here who will translate them.' (In this tactful way he managed to restrain those who enjoy showing off their knowledge of foreign languages.) Before embarking on this 'working' part of the evening Grotowski politely but firmly requested the photo-reporters and television crews to leave the hall.

A recollection came to me of fragments of the very personal words of Andre Gregory four years earlier concerning his wife Chiquita

who had died a year before that. In this way history turned full circle, because the basis of discussion with Grotowski was a film made by Chiquita Gregory in 1989 – the only documentation of the *Action* created by the participants in the work in Pontedera.

How was this film on *Action* made? Richards spoke about it. First of all, the film might be shown only in the presence of Grotowski or himself, for people interested in the activity of the Workcenter from an artistic or research point of view. It followed that the film was not to be used for promotional or commercial purposes or shown on the mass media. It was made when Grotowski realised that the time had come to record what had been done so far. (Richards invariably referred to Grotowski as 'Mr Grotowski' or 'Grotowski', without any familiarity or personal feelings – as if to underline the professional nature of their relationship, despite the closeness they must have achieved and their importance to each other after so many years of work together.)

As a person suitable for creating such a document, Grotowski approached Chiquita Gregory. She accepted. When she arrived with her crew in Italy the difficulties began. Grotowski did not agree to the standard working procedure of the crew – that is, moving amongst the performers, shooting particular moments, interrupting and repeating sequences – because such interferences would harm the balance and whole structure of the process. There was only one way out: the camera shooting the same action, but from different points in the workspace every day.

However, the recording of sound over several days was not to be part of the game: the sound-track had to be a recording of the action on only one day. So the same happened as had occurred several years earlier with the recording of Teatr Laboratorium's *Constant Prince*. The sound recorded on one day was in perfect sync with the pictures shot on other days.

Richards strongly emphasized that both Chiquita Gregory and her crew had been extraordinarily 'delicate' during the recording. Both he and Grotowski underlined several times that what we were going to see was not a performance and should not be received from such a perspective. As it turned out later, despite being reminded of this fact, the power of one's thought habits proved to be stronger than the recollection of these statements.

The film is divided into three parts. The first is a recording of preparation – that is, the realization, under Richards's direction, of those fragments of *Action* which had lacked something on the previous day. The preparation was filmed on only one day and in this way it was a whole and not a compilation of shots of preparation from several days. Therefore the character of preparation expressed was more revealing than the making of a montage of elements for show which 'came off best'.

The second part of the film was of the *Action*, and is very difficult for me to describe. Terms connected with the description of theatre performance emerge for obvious reasons, but they would be out of place here. I start from undisputable facts: the action lasted about forty minutes; five people, including a dark-skinned woman, took part. For the rest, it becomes the more difficult in that I watched this recording through my knowledge of the actuality.

Undoubtedly some elements of the *Action* could belong to theatre performance – the performers sang songs which in some way provoked their movement. . . . However the whole would be difficult to see as a theatre piece. It does not seem to me that we were taken through any kind of 'story' that conformed to any structure of fiction. From my point of view it would be difficult to say that the *Action* had, from the begining, a concrete and given motif or theme which was later developed or resolved in some way.

At most there were some kinds of 'microstories'. One which imprinted itself most strongly on my mind was the transformation of a girl into an old woman – her total change of voice and walk. I didn't have the impression that the *Action* embodied any kind of logic that could be perceived by the spectators; undoubtedly, however, an 'inner logic' existed that was clear for the participants of the action.

Several hundred years of the 'discharming of the world' (in Weberian terms) has resulted in our predisposition to view all that is performed by people in movement as a 'theatre presentation' – a fragment of activity which, to a greater or lesser extent, corresponds with the 'normal' activity of life. Something must be either art or life. From here arises a problem, for example, with the 'art of primitive tribes', where the objects are not created for aesthetic contemplation but presented as such to westerners in galleries and museums.

Attempts made by various creators to blend art into life have frequently become only the aestheticizing of the mediocre. Is what Grotowski was here doing an attempt at the 'next enchantment of the world'? I don't know. He himself says that he is a link in the 'chain' which continues through centuries and sometimes disappears, only to reappear unexpectedly in an entirely different place: he draws, he says, from what has been woven through centuries and revived from time to time in different cultures. Obviously the *Action* had been continuously developing, and what was seen in Wrocław was different from what had been recorded in 1989. The last part of the film contained an explanation given by Grotowski that was quite similar to what we had heard already.

After the film, which was supposed to be the starting point for discussion, there was a break. I got the impression that with the end of the break ended the time of protection for Grotowski as honourable guest. The first question, asked in a very aggressive tone, concerned the inclusion of Richards in the ensemble and the absence of the woman who performed in the film whose energy was deemed much better. The question revealed an inability to break with thinking habits – thinking in categories of a theatre ensemble – in which some creators perform better than others, who should be removed.

Richards answered without any indication of personal affront that they were really sorry that the woman had decided to leave. A condition of their work at the Workcenter was that whoever joined was obliged to work there for at least a year, during which time they had to support themselves. Sometimes, in Italy, they simply could not afford it for a longer period of time and sometimes they simply felt that the time to go had arrived. He, Richards, did not yet feel that his time to go had come.

The following questions were collected by Grotowski, a few at the time, and answered as a batch: but quite frequently a question was used as a pretext for Grotowski to talk about what he wanted to say. He passed on the majority of questions concerning the present work in the Workcenter to Richards.

From this year there was to be a new name for the centre in Pontedera – the Workcenter of Jerzy Grotowski and Thomas Richards. When it became clear to the participants that Richards was now assuming so important a role in the work defined as 'Grotowski's', I got the impression that he was no longer perceived by them in so favourable a light. The parts of the evening concerning Richards came to resemble an exam taken in front of a not-too-sympathetic council of a few hundred. 'Let's see if the one here is fit to be the successor of our Master. It is true that we can attack Grotowski, but he is and will always be ours. The other one here is not.' That would be a quick way of describing the bias of Richards's questioners.

One of the questions concerned the kind of man Richards was and what he did before he got involved with Grotowski. He responded that he came from an 'artistic' family, that one of his parents was a musician and the other an actor, and that one of his grandfathers was a conductor of music. As a consequence he grew up convinced that he would either be an actor or a musician. He plays a number of instuments and has graduated from an acting school. He loved to improvise and it was said that he was good at it. But he was missing something.

Then he met Grotowski, who turned his view of himself upside down. Grotowski claimed that Richards improvised, reached something, got bored with it, and so started all over again. They began work together and Richards started to change. Working on vibratory songs he felt that he came closer to his Jamaican roots (his family on his father's side comes from Jamaica). In the songs he found something very close to him, like his grandmother's songs – despite the fact that he had never heard any of them. For now he is happy doing what he is doing. He said things which could be read in his books and didn't make any more 'intimate' disclosures. He talked mainly about the work.

Richards said that on one day he entered the work room where he trained and found many objects arranged on the floor by Grotowski. He was supposed to do the same 'partiture' as he always did up to this time, moving amongst the obstacles.

Grotowski added that people from the West imagine trance to be total insanity, an immersion in the uncontrollable, which results in some kind of uncoordinated gestures. Real trance, as understood by primal cultures, is something completely different. Different obstacles are thrown underfoot to check if a man is in a real trance. If he avoids them it means that he does not pretend. If he trips over them it means that he is not in a trance. We would commonly think precisely the opposite – but real trance is a form of total concentraton, of not losing oneself. Richards was asked in what way the songs used in *Action* were found. He didn't want to give a precise answer. He said only that they were unusually ancient and came from different cultures.

At one point a question was asked which made Grotowski very angry. More or less, it was: 'If this is a myth what would be the name of God?' Grotowski's reaction was unusually violent. Angrily, he announced that he did not feel the need to name the Higher Power. The questioner stood up and retorted, also angrily: 'I expected such an answer', and left the room. Grotowski said that he believed that there was some kind of Higher Being. He never wanted to give it a name. He always created his own terminology, and when it became common he would leave it and begin to use new words.

As a child he wanted to read the gospels. For this wish he was beaten by a priest. Evangelical texts were lent him secretly by a vicar. In our Catholic Christian country Grotowski had to read the Bible somewhere in an attic. Today he says that this is how it should be read. Jesus was then for him his friend. He was also a friend to a blind horse in the neigbourhood. In contrast to Richards, Grotowski allowed himself a few moments of personal honesty during the evening.

Some of those gathered there were clearly demonstrating their personal relationship to Grotowski – that he was privately somebody important to them. For example, the question was asked: 'Do you remember the important thing you told me a few years back when I met you in the Old Town in Wrocław?' In the question was a hidden regret – that somebody who once said something so important could not be kept in check and could do things that departed from our idea of what he should be doing.

The same young man had earlier asked Grotowski a personal question which he gave him the option of not answering. 'The question' turned out to be an unarticulated howl. Grotowski said with humour that he would not reply to a question posed in such a way. In such situations I always wonder if I am dealing with an unrefined joker, an authentic psychiatric case, or a man who does perceive reality differently, and believes in little intersubjective ways of communication.

There was a question posed which was quite important for people like me who knew Grotowski's work only from what he had written – namely, to what extent they may benefit from his works. Grotowski's answer was that he didn't know. He said that his texts were mainly taken down from occasions when he talked. Later on he only made 'corrections' for clarity. His advice to those who read his old texts was to focus on the practical dimension because only this, according to him, was essential and worth pursuing.

During the evening there emerged a 'call for accountability'. Grotowski was attacked for moralizing now whereas earlier he had himself been a member of the communist Polish Youth Association and the Polish United Party of Workers – the party of communist power in Poland. Furthermore, he had persuaded the whole ensemble to join the party. He answered that all of it was calculated. He knew that the system would go but that he would be too old by then to do anything. His theatre was constantly in danger of being closed down. He summoned his colleagues and asked everyone to join the party so that even if the theatre should be closed down it would be impossible to liquidate its party connection.

The actors showed a certain resistance to this. Zbigniew Cynkutis, for example, was reluctant because, among other reasons, his father had died at the hands of the Soviets in

Katyń. Grotowski's response to this was: 'Is what we are doing now against the murder of Polish officers or not?' Cynkutis said that it was, and in this way was convinced. Grotowski said that being a member of the party was purely instrumental – a means of existing within the system.

His message to the young people present was to do everything in order to reach their goal. Since the main barrier at the moment was not the lack of freedom of speech but lack of finance, everything that sponsors desired should be promised to them despite knowing the impossibility of keeping such promises. The question was asked whether, if 'the country called him back', he would like to return. And Grotowski diplomatically replied that since, at the moment, it hadn't there was no point in thinking about this. There was a question about his future plans. Grotowski answered with brutal honesty that he planned to die.

Luckily, despite the late hour, we didn't descend to questions concerning zodiacal signs. However there was the following: 'How is Easter celebrated in Pontedera?' The answer: 'Any way one wants'.

There was talk about Grotowski's recent enrolment on the list of professors at the Collège de France – the second Pole to be so honoured, the first having been the Polish romantic poet Adam Mickiewicz. Grotowski answered that in one of his conversations with a professor of this honoured Parisian educational institution there was a reference to our great bard. The professor vaguely recalled that there had been some trouble connected with his mystical tendencies.

One of the interesting issues for the conference participants was that of recruitment to the Workcenter. This was addressed by Richards, who said that every year they had hundreds of applicans from among whom they chose only a few. The chosen people come from the field of perfomative art, which is in some way the closest to what is done in Pontedera. Besides having to commit themselves for at least a year and support themselves for this period, they work for six days a week and a dozen or so hours a day.

For some time they had been inviting some theatre groups with whom a specific exchange took place. The guests show their performances and they their *Action*. Maybe, I thought, this was a cause for the continued misunderstanding concerning Grotowski's and Richards's work – the perception of it as another form of theatre show, something to be watched, something composed as a performance.

The meeting in the Theatre Polski lasted for seven hours. At about two in the morning the weariness on both sides became acute. Grotowski said what he had already said; people repeatedly asked him the same questions. The meeting closed with a traditional 'thank you' from Grotowski which made clear that this was indeed the end.

It was good to have had a chance to learn about the present work of one who had once been the most controversial and among the greatest theatre creators in Poland. I get the impression that what he said will reanimate old controversies.

Translated by Jolestic Cynkutis

NTQ Reports and Announcements

Aleks Sierz

NT 2000: the Need to Make Meaning

THE NATIONAL THEATRE'S best-kept secret of 1999 was NT 2000, a year-long series of 45-minute public platforms that staged extracts from the 'hundred most significant plays of the century', along with discussions involving writers, directors, and actors, many from original productions. Although the plays were selected by quite a small number of theatre practitioners – about 850 were asked to nominate ten plays each – the producer Angus MacKechnie says that it was an essentially 'democratic' process. When all the results were analysed, 188 writers had been nominated for 377 plays. Overall, Miller garnered the most votes, followed closely by Pinter and Beckett. The top five plays were *Waiting for Godot, Death of a Salesman, A Streetcar Named Desire, Look Back in Anger,* and *Long Day's Journey into Night.*

MacKechnie's methodology does raise many questions: although he wanted 'significant' rather than 'best' plays, his criteria also encouraged people to include 'plays that you have enjoyed'. Thus postmodern relativism jostled with 'great, influential, or important' work, and objections abounded. Just how significant are Ena Lamont Stewart's *Men Should Weep* (1947) or August Wilson's *Fences* (1985) in a list that has excluded Jones and Pinero, Lonsdale and Greene, Whiting and Simpson, Mercer and Rudkin, Murphy and Wood, Marcus and Halliwell, Matura and Pinnock? *The Mousetrap* is certainly significant, but is it great or influential? How many people actually voted for *Dry Rot* or *Run for Your Wife*? Even more problematic were the 1990s: no mention of Sarah Kane's *Blasted*, Mark Ravenhill's *Shopping and Fucking*, or *Trainspotting*. Like all such surveys, NT 2000 is a snapshot of reputation rather than quality.

The decision to represent each playwright with only one play was also problematic. Pinter is thus represented by *The Caretaker* rather than *The Birthday Party*, Orton by *Loot* rather than *What the Butler Saw*, Hare by *Racing Demon* rather than *Plenty*. Limiting the list to English drama worldwide resulted in 79 entries coming from Great Britain and Ireland (nine Irish, four Scottish, one Welsh), twenty from North America, one from South Africa – but none from Australia or New Zealand. Only fourteen writers were women and

three black, but this reflects the social history of production rather than today's prejudice.

However, because many of those voting were connected with the National, the list was swelled by its own past productions: how else could Tony Harrison's *The Trackers of Oxyrhynchus* (National, 1990) be one of the hundred great plays of the century? Alan Bennett is an important writer, but is *The Madness of George III* (National, 1991) his most significant work? Would Sophie Treadwell's *Machinal* (1928) have made the list if not for the recent National revival? Is Tony Kushner's *Angels in America* (National, 1993) really the ninth most significant play of the century?

By excluding plays in translation (no Chekhov, Brecht, or Pirandello), NT 2000 says less about theatre history than about a mythical English heritage. But limiting selections to an English-language tradition did have the advantage of a tighter focus. It allowed some rarely performed plays – Kaufman and Hart's *Once in a Lifetime* (1930), Lorraine Hansbury's *A Raisin in the Sun* (1959), and Heathcote Williams's *AC/DC* (1970) – to creep in. But it also meant that the platforms captured the self-referential quality of theatre. Noël Coward's *Private Lives* (1930), for example, was echoed by Patrick Marber's *Closer* (1997), with *Educating Rita* referring back to *Pygmalion*, and *Observe the Sons of Ulster* to *Oh What a Lovely War!*

So while the list did fairly represent the grand sweep of English-language theatre, dominated by the great mid-century American tragedies along with Pinter and Beckett, it also tended to be more reflective of the Irish contribution (from J. M. Synge to Conor McPherson) than to the Scots (from J. M. Barrie to C. P. Taylor), and – despite examples from the Manchester School – valued the metropolis over the regions. Few would quarrel with the most popular selections; but even fewer would agree with the more idiosyncratic choices.

But whatever doubts arose about the list, the platforms themselves were often revelatory. Hampered by the fact that authors, directors, and cast members had already died, those platforms covering the earlier part of the century were more academic than the later ones. Even so, the blessing of longevity allowed the 86-year-old politician Barbara Castle to be present on the platform for Galsworthy's *Strife* (1909), a play in which she had acted during the 1920s.

The importance of NT 2000 – apart from its frank celebration of theatre – lay in its emphasis on public discussion as a means of widening the audience for a play and clarifying its meaning. This was particularly apt for two platforms where the authors, Edward Bond and Howard Barker, refused permission (because of ongoing conflicts with the National) for extracts from their plays to be used. Instead, there were discussions on 'Theatre and Censorship' and 'Theatre and the Establishment'.

The testimony of original cast members was always revealing. In the platform on *Oh What a Lovely War!* actor Murray Melvin pointed out that far from being forced to introduce a happy ending for the West End transfer of the play, Joan Littlewood was robustly cheerful about the prospect, apparently saying: 'Let's give 'em what they want.' Patricia Franklin, who was in the Royal Court revival of Bond's *Saved*, stressed the fact that the pram in the baby-stoning scene was completely empty, without even a doll, which testifies to the power of theatre to stir audience imaginations. In Barker's *Victory*, the sound of seats slamming as people walked out during the play's aggressively obscene opening exchanges was taped and used in the soundtrack of the subsequent revival.

The fact that Caryl Churchill pioneered the use of overlapping dialogue in *Top Girls* (1982) is well known; but director Max Stafford-Clark pointed out that although this worked well in a smallish theatre such as the Royal Court, the overlapping lines tended to blur in bigger Broadway theatres. Original cast members of *Top Girls* also remembered how New York audiences were less inhibited than London ones in their hunger to discuss the play with the actors after the show.

It explains much about the structure of Jim Cartwright's *Road* (1986) to know that it grew from an end-of-year drama school monologue. Edward Tudor-Pole, who played Scullery in the first production, also commented on the hazards of promenade performances: his offer of a drink from an open bottle was taken up by one audience member, who took a swig and immediately announced: 'It's water!' It was also worth being reminded that the first audiences for *Bent* (1979) did not know that the play was set in Hitler's Germany, and so were shocked when stormtroopers crashed into the seemingly ordinary living-room during the first scene.

Sometimes the event itself was exemplary. I cannot think of a better confirmation of the cult status of Mike Leigh's *Abigail's Party* (1977) than seeing its original cast (including Alison Steadman) performing extracts to a packed 1,150-seat Olivier Theatre to a wildly enthusiastic audience. Likewise, Peter Barnes talking about the politics of humour in *The Ruling Class* (1968) or Sarah Daniels remembering how she failed to join a militant attack on a sexist shop-window display during the first run of *Masterpieces* (1983) said a lot about each writer.

Since MacKechnie has recorded all the platforms and created an archive of documentation

around the project, NT 2000 will remain a valuable resource. If the project's use of lists and criteria such as significance and personal enjoyment to assess the value of plays makes it typical of its time, perhaps it was also symbolic of something larger: the need for public discussion of the meaning of plays.

The Twin Legacy of the Century

TWO EVENTS IN 1999 forged a distinctive historical connection. On 19 August, the Theatre by the Lake, the last-but-one new producing theatre of the Millennium in Britain, opened at Keswick in Cumbria. In doing so it revived an older tradition, begun when the touring Century Theatre settled on that site in 1976.

Century Theatre was designed in 1947 by John Ridley, an engineer from Hinckley, in Leicestershire. It was intended to be a completely self-contained mobile unit to tour high-standard work, mostly in the Midlands and the North of England. Four ex-service trailers were used as the basis of the theatre, with the main elements constructed out of aluminium.

Overall, the theatre toured in 28 wagons, transporting the stage, auditorium, dressing-rooms, accommodation for the actors, a kitchen, canteen, and a box office, all of which could be assembled in eight hours. The company was run on a co-operative basis, each member being paid the same wage and being expected to double in erecting the theatre, driving the trucks, and cooking meals. The dream of Firmin Gémier and the Théâtre National Ambulant in the early years of the century, to attract audiences by creating excitement in a community as the trucks arrived and a theatre was created in its heart, before the eyes of the inhabitants, was realized.

In its time the Century stage has been crossed and peopled by many distinguished actors – among them Dame Judi Dench, Helen Mirren, and Bob Hoskins. The fund-raising, under the direction of Wilfred Harrison, included donations from many luminaries of the theatrical and other artistic professions, giving the theatre a place in the memories and hearts of many artists. Other help was donated in cash and in kind by Midland firms, giving the Century a special relationship with business in its area.

In 1974, changes in the traffic regulations created great difficulties for the theatre, and in 1976 it put down roots in Keswick, where it continued to be used as the town's theatre until 1996. In that year, Century Theatre came home, to Snibston Discovery Park in Leicestershire – just ten miles or so from Hinckley, where it had been built. The funding included a Lottery grant of £154, 000 and support from local authorities and the Government Single Regeneration Fund.

Snibston Discovery Park is a hands-on learning resource staffed by Leicestershire Museums Arts and Records Service. Other resources on the site include a coal mine, staffed by ex-miners, in which children can experience something of what it was like to work down a pit. The theatre is open to the public, and holds continuous exhibitions, both in the theatre itself and in the adjacent gallery. Guided tours are available on request, and there is a programme of lectures on the history of the theatre.

The official opening – which took the form of a reunion of past members – was on 25 April 1999. In addition to serving as a presenting theatre for touring productions, the new Century Theatre hopes to become a centre of research and scholarship devoted to touring theatre. The first stage is to classify the Century Theatre archive and to construct a sound archive of recorded memories of both performers and audience. Future projects include a census of other sources of material on touring theatre; establishing a website; research into the impact of the theatre on the communities it visited; and further exhibitions and conferences.

Already established as a centre for research which has attracted scholars from this country and the USA, the Century will eventually become the centre for research into travelling theatre.

Contact
Century Theatre, Snibston Discovery Centre,
Ashby Road, Coalville, Leics. LE67 3LN
Telephone: 01530 831863

The Theatre by the Lake

Occupying the same site in Keswick, Theatre by the Lake opened on 19 August 1999. Unlike its predecessor, the new theatre will be an all-the-year-round producing theatre, and although it will still provide a service to the passing, temporary tourist audiences of the summer period, it will largely be providing a continuous service to the population of Cumbria and beyond from what must be a position that has few rivals in the natural beauty of its setting.

The theatre, under the direction of Patric Gilchrist, is a direct offshoot of Century Theatre, the controlling body, Cumbria Theatre Trust, having been established by decision of the Century Theatre's Board of Directors in 1984 to realize the project. The two bodies merged again in 1998.

The new theatre is built of local stone and roofed with local slate, to fit in with the surrounding environment of Derwentwater. It comprises a 400-seat auditorium; an 80-seat studio space; two exhibition spaces; film-screening facilities; rehearsal and meeting rooms for hire; conference facilities; a coffee shop; and fully licensed bars. There is full access for the disabled

There have been many changes in the Lake District since the Century Theatre first played there in 1961, nearly half a century ago. The tourist industry has blossomed and communications have radically developed. The new theatre stands fair to make a major contribution to the cultural and economic life of Cumbria.

Contact
Theatre by the Lake, Keswick, Cumbria, CH12 5DJ
Telephone: 017687 74411

NTQ Book Reviews

edited by Maggie Gale

Johannes Birringer
Media and Performance: along the Border
Baltimore; London: Johns Hopkins University
Press, 1998. £16.50.
ISBN: 0-8018-582-6.

RoseLee Goldberg
Performance: Live Art Since the 'Sixties
London: Thames and Hudson, 1998. £32.00.
ISBN: 0-500-01875-8.

Harold B. Segel
The Body Ascendant:
Modernism and the Physical Imperative
Baltimore; London: Johns Hopkins University
Press, 1998. £30.00.
ISBN: 0-8018-5821-6.

In 1995 Sylvie Guillem presented her own TV
dance series, *Evidentia*. It included a film directed
by Françoise Ha Van entitled *Movement*. The piece
weaves archival footage with newly created film
images, editing them together to form an original
choreography investigating the nature of movement, its rhythm, diversity, beauty, and violence.

Divided into sections, *Movement Nine* contains
a black and white clip lasting no more than 45
seconds in which we see a dancer in 1930s' style
tunic performing exercises on a lawn. The image
slowly pans out to reveal more and more bodies
moving in unison until the single dancer becomes
part of a thousand-strong movement of young
women at the Nüremberg Rallies.

This was the image in my mind as I read the
final chapter of Segel's remarkable study, *Body
Ascendant: Modernism and the Physical Imperative*,
and it is the image which, for me, he deconstructs:
how all too easily the modernist obsession with
the physical could lead to the growth of Nazi
ideology and its terrible and extreme finale.

Segel doesn't really have to try too hard. He
systematically presents the reader with the realities of trends in modernist performance, literature, and philosophy, in the light of the social and
political climate at the end of the nineteenth and
early part of the twentieth century, and the book
seems to forge ahead to an inevitable conclusion.
His arguments are underpinned throughout by
reference to issues of gender and religion. His
analysis is detailed and far-ranging, linking performance disciplines with literature, philosophy,
and physical culture in order to uncover why this
period was so preoccupied with the body, how
this preoccupation manifested itself, and what the

consequences of this were. This is a remarkable
study and one which no one seriously interested
in the history of ideas, developments in art, and
the politics of this century should ignore.

The central area of debate is dance, and its
elevation to a significant art form. In 'The Dance
Phenomenon', he revisits a well-documented area
in order to try and uncover the reasons behind the
powerful influence of dance on the arts and on
culture, and its attraction for so many of the
period's intellectuals. The power of non-verbal
expression and the pursuit of physical excellence
and actual experience are carefully examined.
In six surrounding chapters he emphasizes the
negation of the importance of language and of
rational, cerebral thought, taking a detailed look
at the new non-verbal form of modernist pantomime, discussing dramatists from Chekhov to
Gertrude Stein, and finally extending the debate
to encompass Dadaism.

In a direct comparison with the almost exclusively female-led modern dance movement, Segel
examines the masculine physical experience and
its direct influence on literary style through the
lives and writings of 'men of action' such as
Teddy Roosevelt, Ernest Hemingway, and F. T.
Marinetti. Beginning with Nietszche, he examines
modernist philosophy, moving through Mauthner,
Wittgenstein, and Bergson. He explores physically oriented culture movements, the revival of
the Olympic Games, celebrities who popularized
health and body building, and the rise of mass
youth movements such as the Boy Scouts and the
more insidious Czech Sokol.

Eventually Segel takes a more specific look at
the growth of arguments put forward by writers
against Judaeo-Christian beliefs, from the seeds
sown by Nietszche to Adolf Hitler himself. This
book reminds us that in view of recent global
events we may not really have moved on at all.
The Body Ascendant demonstrates the importance
of remembering – remembering both the achievements of modernism and also its dark side.

Modernism elevated the body. Dance became,
in Segel's words, 'the non-verbal expression of
powerful emotions buried deep within the
psyche' – and the body has continued to be an
important site for discourse throughout the
twentieth century. Johannes Birringer's recent
work *Media and Performance: across the Border*, also
uses dance and the body as the central axiom
from which to discuss the wider implications
for performance practice of being part of an
increasingly technologized world. In the preface

to this lengthy and difficult publication, Birringer states that he is offering us a 'body of thinking': i.e., 'a consciousness of performance based on physical practices and a conceptual knowledge of theatre, dance, video, and performance art'.

The book looks at the relationship between media technologies and cyberspace (a term borrowed from William Gibson) and performance. Birringer identifies media technologies as video technology, broadcast television, MTV, digital music sampling, and computer processing. Discussing both the impact on performance practices of these areas and the divide between them, he offers an interior view informed by his own performance practice and research and also his particular interest in dance- and body-oriented practices. This he sees as pertinent to the current obsession with virtual bodies and cyberspace, with its inference of the displacement of the physical body and actual human contact. From the beginning, he sets up a dialogue between the actual and the virtual, believing that, whether it be conscious or unconscious, our involvement as artists and our embodiment of practice has a potential for activism as well as reaction. The book takes on the responsibility of the politics of performance.

The introductory chapter, entitled, 'This is the Theatre That Was to Be Expected and Foreseen', necessarily gives his perspective on recent performance history, and identifies trends in contemporary performance practice through an analysis of both theories of performance and an extensive range of productions, multicultural and multidisciplinary, large- and small-scale. While acknowledging theory's debt to performance and performance's debt to the visual arts art from Duchamp onwards., he also notes the death of theatre (traditional text-based drama), citing both contemporary postmodern theories and their irrelevance to his life and education. His global and inclusive outlook pervades a publication which highlights community and activist work – art that mends and motivates across cultural, political, and social borders.

The book is divided into four sections – 'Dancing with Technologies', 'Impossible Anatomies', 'Culture in Action', and 'Virtual Communities' – transversed by nine chapters. Each chapter is further subdivided, under headings such as 'Dancing on the Edges', 'Body Spaces', 'Between Physical Theatre', 'Virtual Reality'. I'm not sure how helpful this information is to the potential reader except to underline the complexities of the debate and of the author's thought process. *Media and Performance* was six years in the making, and continually interweaves analysis of performance events with analysis of changing practices in the process toward performance, generated by the development of and the artists' relationship towards media technologies. This Birringer does in equal measure by investigating both the work of movement/dance artists (with an emphasis on European Tanztheatre), artists specifically working with technology (from video to CD-ROM), his own research and practice with the collective performance group Alien Nation Co., and investigative workshops entitled 'Lively Bodies Lively Machines'.

In some ways the book appears like packaging for publication of Birringer's own research, and having never seen the work it is difficult to assess its quality and therefore its value. I have also some personal reservations and disagreements surrounding his reading of many artists and their works. Nevertheless, through this analysis he continually develops theory and comments upon the evolving and emerging new theories of other critics. As readers we embark on a journey with the author through his personal landscape. The emphasis is on the experience of the practitioner and how he or she subsequently locates his or her work, developing theory from this experience.

Although Birringer's wordiness and seemingly deliberately clever (often alienating) style can be irritating, I did relish his ability to be highly critical both of his own work and that of others. He is never sycophantic towards technology, and maintains a healthy questioning of the relevance to performance of digital advances, clearly seeing where these are truly integrated into performance practice and where the gap is still too wide. This is especially so in relation to computer technology and dance (digital dancing), where sight is often lost of the human relevance because of over-excitement about the 'sexiness' of the medium. Here his main worry is that we are 'leaving the body behind', and his description of his dance in cyberspace utilizing VR technology clearly demonstrates his point.

He also warns against mass consumerism encroaching upon certain artworks and the spaces (galleries, museums, theatres) which house them. Birringer looks at the history and the present state of 'virtual communities' and warns against the increasing ownership of web space and indeed of the media in general by huge multinational corporations. From his perspective, art work has been and always will be about bodily experience and about empowering the individual – commenting upon the social fabric of our society and instigating the possibilities of positive change for displaced and disenfranchised groups. This is emphasized through a fascinating investigation of the work of Chicago-based Street Level Video – the book is worth having just for this.

The (inevitable) integration of new media and technology must be grasped and directed towards the good of these art experiences and not, as is the danger, overshadow, overtake, and further increase the cultural and social divide. Communities and artists must re-appropriate and re-possess technology to enhance their aims. To quote the author: 'I still have enormous difficulties in accepting the vision being promoted of a fully realized technological society, since it avoids answering any serious questions about the power relations between technology and people, the design and distribution of information and its alternative use by different social factors or communities, and the survival of living bodies despite the violence of those final abstractions.' This underlines the seriousness of the debate Birringer has begun, however one feels about the analysis of specific artists and styles.

Does a debate always need to be accomplished with words? As I have suggested, Birringer's text can often be alienating – especially, I fear, to students of the arts. Perhaps body-oriented art practices need new forms to mediate them? Furthermore, experimental performance work can be elusive, and even with more traditional dance work the live experience is hard to relay. As educators and artists we need to encourage and excite the next generation of artists to invent new forms and move outside the constraints of present practice.

RoseLee Goldberg's new book, *Performance: Live Art since the 'Sixties*, can help us do just that. It also presents us with a way in which to remember which is as relevant to its era as Segel's is to his. The sequel to *Performance Art: from Futurism to the Present*, the highly regarded and hugely popular text published originally in 1979, some of the work included in this new book crosses over with the final chapter of its predecessor; for this, too, is also a critical history of a 'hybrid' genre, but one which emphasizes the visual, and the immediate impact of the photograph over text as the most pertinent medium through which to remember and in some way keep alive ephemeral performance/live art events in time.

Possibly due to the increase in practitioners in the field of performance, Goldberg has chosen a structure which is neither chronological nor geographical. Instead she divides the work into thematic chapters, allowing the reader/viewer to achieve a globally and temporally encompassing picture of part of the huge body of work that forms the recent history of performance. It is the layout of the chapters and individual pages, the way photographs have been chosen and displayed in relation or juxtaposition to each other, that acts as the critical medium. Each double-page spread is carefully designed, resulting in a striking resonance amongst the various art works/events portrayed. The accompanying notes to each image give just enough information, especially when taken in conjunction with an articulate introduction, allowing the reader to enjoy his or her own perspective and 'insert between the lines'.

The book opens with a brief foreword by Laurie Anderson, whose own work spans the last three decades and who can provide a welcome artist's view. In it she stresses how she has come to value the importance of keeping a visual record of events in order to keep one's work from disappearing or being distorted by time and memory. There then follows an introduction by Goldberg in which she gives a brief history, attempts to define some of the emergent genres, and explains the reasons behind her choice of presentation. As she herself states: 'Each picture carries the residue of time, and each has a way of making the past and the present fleetingly real.'

Each of the six chapters opens with a short introduction of its own, explaining the chosen contextualization. Chapter One, 'Performance, Politics, Real Life', looks at happenings and events by radical performance artists and groups such as Fluxus, Joseph Beuys, Alistair Maclennan, Black Market International, Cai Guo Qiang, and Roman Signer. The images denote a shared connection with environment, object, and human presence, in order to comment on and activate psychological, social, and/or political issues. Chapter Two, 'Theatre, Music, Opera', suggests that it was avant-garde artists and musicians such as Cage, Anderson, and Kaprow who transformed the nature of theatrical performance. This chapter has a more theatrical look, as many of the images are from stage productions, but it does not overlook artists such as the Gob Squad, who take theatre into ordinary everyday settings.

Chapter Three, 'The Body: Ritual, Living Sculpture, Performed Photography', looks at the body as both site and laboratory in the work of artists who include Stelarc, Marina Abramovic, Chris Burden, Yoko Ono, and Mariko Mori. It contains often disquieting images from healing and catharsis to endurance and mutilation – the body is art, as art, either transformed or exposed. Chapter Four 'Identities: Feminism, Multiculturalism, Sexuality', discusses the blurring of boundaries between high and low culture, craft and art, and looks at the discovery of sexual and cultural identities – courageous art which breaks social taboos and challenges the social fabric. These pictures, of artists such as Orlan, Annie Sprinkle, David Wojnarowicz, and Isaac Julien show the diversity of our realities as artists and as human beings.

Chapter Five, 'Dance', exposes the obsession of the 'seventies with pure form, of the 'eighties with refinding content, and of the 'nineties with the appropriation of both multi-media and architectural language. The images, some of the most stunning and beautiful in the book, show the continued potency of dance and its incredible diversity. Chapter Six, 'Video, Rock and Roll, the Spoken Word', moves from 'sixties Pop Art to DJ Spooky, charting the incorporation of mass culture and the utilization of visual and sonic technology. Often fun and characterful, the images are of trash and camp, of clubs and parties and cabaret, of film and video works.

Whilst Harold B. Segel conjures up the past through his eloquent prose style and a few well-chosen black and white pictures, Birringer says that he originally conceived his book as a video diary (something to think about for the future there). But RoseLee Goldberg allows the skilled eye of the photographer to tell the stories. I never saw Joseph Beuys's 1965 installation piece *How to Explain Pictures to a Dead Hare*, but the haunting image reproduced in this essential new book ensures its continual impact along with that of the many other art works included.

HEATHER RUTLAND

Susan Wiseman
Drama and Politics in the English Civil War
Cambridge: Cambridge UP, 1998. 297 p.
ISBN: 0-521-47221-0.

In scrutinizing a period too often ignored in accounts of English theatre – that 'gap' between 1642 and 1660 habitually characterized as the result of puritan repression of a drama allied with royalism – Sue Wiseman opens up a topic vital to our understanding both of drama itself and of the question of genre. Beginning with a rereading of the 1642 ordinance which closed the playhouses, she asks why and how plays were implicated in the politics and ideology of the Civil War years, and mounts a well-argued attack on the orthodox view of a 'royalist' drama in abeyance.

In Part One, covering the period 1642 to 1649, she offers a number of case studies which place drama in the context of a wide mixture of genres which 'staged' the public discussion of politics. News pamphlets in dialogue form and popular playlets are examined as hybrid forms, operating at the borders of printed and oral discussion; popular royalism and radicalism are shown to have combined in the pamphlets of Overton and Sheppard; and the case is made for seeing this mix of news and pamphlet activity as constituting 'an emerging sphere of printed dramatic debate'.

Part Two considers a number of dramatists of the 1650s (Cavendish, Shirley, Flecknoe, Davenant, Tatham) to investigate the politics of closet drama, masque, opera, civic shows and pageantry, tragi-comedy, and pastoral. Drama in all its forms was, it is argued, a space in which debates about the new English polity and between competing royalisms could take place. Students and teachers of seventeenth-century drama will find valuable this extension of the re-examination begun by Martin Butler: the book's wider impact, however, should be that it adds to the mounting pressure for a radical rethinking of genre in seventeenth-century culture.

MAUREEN BELL

Peter Bailey
Popular Culture and Performance in the Victorian City
Cambridge: Cambridge UP, 1998, x, 258 p.
ISBN: 0-521-57417-X.

'I exit stage left,' says Peter Bailey at the end of one his chapters, 'with no more than the merest suggestion of the comic singer's knowing wink.' One of the pleasures of re-reading the essays that make up this long-anticipated book, many of them previously published, is that we are allowed to engage at more length with their affable but sometimes elusive author. As his reflective introduction suggests, Bailey's instinctive feel for the vitality of his subject-matter has always been tempered by his respect for methodological rigor; and he has always known that it is as important to tell the story 'from the inside', to be aware of one's own positioning as a social historian, as 'from below', as it felt to ordinary people at the time. Such discriminating attitudes are entirely appropriate to the ripeness – and occasional rankness – of the cultural field he has made his own.

Bailey studies social performance on and off the Victorian stage: he reconstructs the art of music-hall 'swells' like 'Champagne Charlie' and George Leybourne, and he re-animates cartoon characters from the comic papers such as 'Ally Sloper'; he interrogates dodgy impresarios from Billy Holland, 'the Emperor of Lambeth', to George Edwardes, 'the Guv'nor' of the Gaiety; he scrutinizes from a respectful distance the careers of barmaids and chorus girls.

Always he seeks, and generally finds, the modes of self-presentation which made social interaction profitable, pleasurable – and risky. In the case of the more obviously put-upon, this means identifying the opportunities for individual assertion that emerged out of professional exploitation. Bailey's brilliant concept of 'para-sexuality', for instance, makes Foucault look rather jejune, since it combines two possible meanings of the prefix 'para' – 'almost' and 'against' – and sets them against the noun, allowing for codes of behaviour that were simultaneously a modification of and a protection from physical sexuality. Barmaids and other supposedly glamorous trades can thus be seen to have served a 'para-sexual' function in the leisure business; it was their rationale, their burden, their skill, and perhaps their salvation, to represent sexual relations without necessarily carrying them out.

Similarly, Bailey's cunning identification of 'knowingness' as a key component in popular entertainment recognizes the significance of communal competence in audience responses to the class-based sexual conventions that originally operated in the local halls – though by the turn of the century, with increased centralization, 'knowingness' was 'fast becoming a second language for all classes, as music hall itself became an agreeable national *alter ego.'*

In the contemporary academic arena where performance theory, ideological examination, sociological method, and literary discourse interact increasingly with one another, there are plenty of opportunities for the multi-talented intellectual, but no one does it better or with more appealing subtlety than Peter Bailey.

JOHN STOKES

Helen Gilbert, ed.
(Post) Colonial Stages: Critical and Creative Views on Drama, Theatre and Performance
Hebden Bridge: Dangaroo, 1999. 279 p. £14.95.
ISBN: 1-871-04953-9.

(Post) Colonial Stages has set itself – and, in many respects, has managed to meet – a very broad and impressive remit within a critical field that has been rather sadly overlooked by much theatre and performance study. A useful collection for both scholars and students, it includes Gilbert's succinct introduction; eighteen previously unpublished critical essays on colonial and post-colonial drama, theatre, and performance by some of the field's leading critics; three examples of performance material (two excerpts and one complete short play); and one interview, with Aotearoa/New Zealand playwright Hone Kouka.

The critical essays range historically from the nineteenth century to the present, and geographically, across Africa, Australasia, North America, the Caribbean, and Ireland. And the creative performance texts come from Native American William S. Yellow Robe, Jr., Jamaican theatre collective Sistren, and Singapore playwright Chin Woon Ping. As Gilbert points out in her introduction, theatre and performance studies offer an exceptional field within which colonial and post-colonial studies can further their considerations of relations of power which are not only literary, but also spatial, embodied, and temporal. In this respect *(Post) Colonial Stages* offers some compelling readings of popular cultural events (including Sheila Rabillard's nuanced consideration of the opening of the Fifteenth Commonwealth Games in Victoria, British Columbia, in 1994), although it is still rather drama-oriented (with six essays focusing on one or two plays).

Theatre and performance studies, too, can benefit from the ideologically committed premises of post/colonial study. This comes across in the authors' analyses of issues of nationalism, race, cultural identity and sovereignty, and gender. The book is usefully indexed and, although full and productive as it stands, might have further benefited the field (and the reader new to this field) from the inclusion of a subject bibliography.

JENNIFER HARVIE

Vasili Osipovich Toporkov, trans. Christine Edwards
Stanislavski in Rehearsal: the Final Years
New York: Routledge, 1998. 224 p.
ISBN: 0-87830-091-0.

This reprint of *Stanislavski in Rehearsal* is a fascinating and honest account of his work on three particular productions: *The Embezzlers*, *Dead Souls*, and *Tartuffe*. The author of this account is actor Vasili Toporkov, a member of the 'laboratory' of actors working with Stanislavski towards the end of his life in the 1930s. Toporkov confronts the problems of implementing Stanislavski's continually developing method with candour and humour, rendering the account an immensely enjoyable and informative read.

The book begins with an overview of actor training as experienced by Toporkov both at the Imperial Alexandrinsky Theatre in Petersburg and later at the Moscow Art Theatre. This presents an informed perspective on what exactly *was* so innovative about Stanislavski's approach to acting in comparison with his contemporaries. Perhaps one of the most significant aspects of this book is the insider's insight into the Method of Physical Actions. This Method is possibly one of the least understood areas of Stanislavski's work for us in the West, particularly as it seems to contradict much of the previous text-based analytical work proposed by Stanislavski in the earlier stages of his system.

As well as providing us with an honest account of a young actor's struggle with the Method, the book is full of pithy epigrams presented as Stanislavski's direct speech. This is an extremely useful book for actors, directors, students, or teachers who wish to understand more comprehensively the final stages of Stanislavski's system, as well as the strengths and difficulties of implementing the Method of Physical Actions. It also provides great insights into Stanislavski's vivid imagination as a *director* with specific reference to the three texts cited.

BELLA MERLIN

Richard Boon and Jane Plastow, eds.
Theatre Matters:
Performance and Culture on the World Stage
Cambridge: Cambridge UP, 1998. 203 p. £35.00.
ISBN: 0-521-63054-1.

As the title suggests, this collection starts from the rather unfashionable premise that theatre matters, and that it plays a vital role in the political and cultural struggles of oppressed peoples throughout the world. However, the strength of this collection is not simply that it reaffirms the power of theatre for the benefit of the jaded western academic. As Paul Heritage comments in his contribution, 'The Promise of Performance', the practice of theatre in colonial and post-colonial societies has already become something of a touchstone for those interested in the efficacy of political theatre. The essays in this collection demonstrate that, in reality, theatrical practice in these societies is far more complex and contingent than the conventional image suggests.

Ian Steadman argues that the theatre of post-apartheid South Africa needs to break free from the notion of a simplified, essential Africanness; Femi Osofisan discusses the sheer difficulty of writing and producing oppositional theatre in a military dictatorship. Christopher Innes, Carole-Ann Upton, and George Woodyard contribute essays on the role of the playwright who speaks (or attempts to speak) for his or her society in Canada, the Caribbean, and Argentina.

The picture painted in these essays (and in others in the collection) is of a network of theatre practices that are not grounded in anything as simple as an underlying ideology; rather, they demonstrate that theatre is always inextricably bound up with social practice, and that it is at its most effective (and its most useful) when it responds to specific social situations, rather than to a more diffuse idea of general social injustice. This collection will be of considerable interest to academics and postgraduates interested in post-colonial theatre.

DAVID PATTIE

Simon Shepherd
Studying Plays
London: Arnold, 1998. 184 p. £10.99.
ISBN 0-340-70571-X.

As an introduction to the analysis of the dramatic text this is a curiously uneven book, though the scarcity of such material must make it welcome. It is divided into six sections: 'Getting Started', 'Character and Persons', 'Dialogue, Plot, Action, and the Actor's Body', 'Spaces', and 'Culture and Interpretation'. Each section has clearly titled sub-divisions which make consultation straightforward. The unevenness of the book lies in the inconsistency of the assumptions made about its readership: some sections are apparently aimed at A-Level Theatre Studies students, whilst others assume odd leaps of logic in the reader's basic knowledge.

My undergraduate students considered this a useful book to know about at the beginning of a degree, but found the discussion of specific play-texts disappointing. The omission of extracts from the plays discussed in detail is a mistake – the project underscores the need to develop specific interpretive skills when reading plays, but a closer examination of textual exemplars would have grounded the overall analysis and made it more student-friendly.

MARY LUCKHURST

Ramsey Burt
Alien Bodies: Representations of Modernity, Race, and Nation in Early Modern Dance
London; New York: Routledge, 1998.

As the cover of Ramsey Burt's *Alien Bodies* declares, his *The Male Dancer* (1995) was 'highly acclaimed', and with good cause. It is a hard act for *Alien Bodies* to follow. Again, Burt has chosen to investigate a relatively familiar area from an original standpoint. However, the premise on which the new book is based is more complex, and, as Burt himself admits in the introduction, it is not a 'straightforward' one. This is arguably a result of the writing rather than the subject matter. Burt strenuously resists engaging with postmodern theory, yet even the thesis of the book reflects a postmodern sensitivity for stories and the 'other'.

This tension produces needless, increasingly irritating reiterations of the direction and focus of the argument which nevertheless fail to contribute to clarity or cohesion. Adoption of a post-modern paradigm at the outset could have released an exciting exploration of discontinuity and commonality in disparate stories of modern dancing bodies.

But representations of modernity, especially those traditionally excluded, certainly require serious examination. Burt offers this, and succeeds in furthering a re-formation of the modern dance canon. Yet there is surely more that ought to be said about modern dancers and their dances on other stages.

FIONA WARNE